WHO'S HAVING THIS BABY?

WHO'S HAVING THIS BABY?

Perspectives on Birthing

By
Helen M. Sterk, Carla H. Hay, Alice Beck Kehoe,
Krista Ratcliffe, and Leona VandeVusse

Michigan State University Press
East Lansing

Copyright © 2002 Michigan State University Press
◯ The paper used in this publication meets the minimum requirements of
ANSI/NISO Z39.48–1992 (R 1997) (Permanence of Paper).

Michigan State University Press
East Lansing, Michigan 48823–5202

Printed and bound in the United States of America.

08 07 06 05 04 03 02   1 2 3 4 5 6 7

LIBRARY OF CONGRESS CATALOGING-IN-PUBLICATION DATA

Who's having this baby? : perspectives on birthing / By Helen M. Sterk [et al.].

   p. cm.
Includes bibliographical references.
 ISBN 0-87013-615-1 (pbk. : alk. paper)
 1. Childbirth—History. 2. Childbirth—Cross-cultural studies. 3. Childbirth in
literature. 4. Midwifery—History. 5. Women patients—Civil rights. 6. Women's
rights. I. Sterk, Helen M., 1952-
 GN482.1 .W48 2002
 618.4'09—dc21   2002001585

Cover design by Heather Truelove
Book design by Michael J. Brooks

Visit Michigan State University Press on the World Wide Web at:
www.msupress.msu.edu

CONTENTS

WE SEE THE WOMEN

An Introduction

Helen M. Sterk

I became pregnant at age thirty-five. Defined as an elderly first-time mother, I became afraid something would go terribly wrong. So, I haunted bookstores, looking for books that would tell me women's stories, that would show me how they survived. At a very basic level, I wanted to know how they lived through labor and delivery. I could not imagine how a person could endure having a child emerge from her body.

As a result of my search, I found that American culture in general cannot imagine how a woman could come through birth, either. American culture can imagine a doctor delivering a baby, a nurse managing a woman's care, even a midwife guiding the birthing process, but not what a woman experiences. As far as cultural messages go, when we look at and talk about birth, we see and hear the experts (Sterk 1996).

In this book, however, we see the women.

Motivated by a desire to understand birth from the point of view of the people who experience it most intimately, over the last decade I have been developing an archive, called The Birthing Project, of women's stories. Held at the Memorial Library at Marquette University in Milwaukee, Wisconsin, this archive soon will contain 131 birthing stories. Of those, 103 are the result of interviews that I have personally conducted and 8 more are the result of interviews I have supervised. Alice Kehoe, anthropologist and author of one of the chapters in this book, conducted 5 interviews on and near American Indian reservations. A friend and colleague, Alice Deakins, an English professor at William Paterson College, taped the stories of three Chinese women while on a trip to China. In addition, Leona VandeVusse, director of the midwifery program at Marquette University and also an author of one this book's chapters, contributed the 15 interviews that form the data for her chapter. All interviews are complete; not all yet are transcribed.

We each asked a series of open-ended questions designed to elicit narratives of experience. The women were promised that their interviews would remain anonymous, their names turned into pseudonyms and all proper names masked by initials. The questions included: What was your prenatal experience like? What sort of care did you receive? What was your labor and delivery like? And what advice do you have for women giving birth? These questions prompted hours and hours of stories. Given that many of the women had more than one baby, we have gathered the stories of more than three hundred births.

The women varied in significant ways. They ranged in age from nineteen to ninety-five at the tine of the interview. Geographically, they lived in clusters of places: New York and New Jersey, Michigan and Wisconsin, central Florida, Montana, California, and China. Yet even though they currently resided in these places, they gave birth all over the world, in the Netherlands, France, Canada, Saudi Arabia, and Libya, as well as the United States. Ethnicities represented include Caucasian, Native American, African American, and Asian, with Caucasian predominating. Their birth experiences ranged from uncomplicated home births to routine hospital births to stillbirths to water births to complicated, life-and-death situations. Caregivers included doctors, nurses, midwives (licensed as well as unlicensed, lay as well as certified nurse midwives), doulas, spouses, partners, and lactation consultants. Some found birthing to be one of the most significant acts they ever had completed, while others were delighted to have been sedated throughout the entire event. Some were married, some not. Some went through severe postpartum depression. Some threw up during the entire pregnancy. In brief, these interviews do a fair, if not entirely complete, job of representing the range of birthing options and experiences available to women living in America in the late twentieth century.

These stories reveal the meanings women associate with giving birth. Becoming "mother" means as many different things as there are different women. It means finally experiencing an orgasm; humiliation from being bound to bed, having to use a bedpan, and being shaved; tremendous joy at the birth of a long-anticipated daughter or son; heart-wrenching sorrow at the death of a baby; deep bonding with a husband who helped to birth the baby at home; resentment at botched episiotomies that limit sexual sensation; pleasure at touching a baby's head crowning between legs; joy at pulling a baby out of one's own body. And on, and on.

These particularities, known only by women giving birth, are lost in literature produced by observers. In that literature, the normal, the expected, is plotted. What is lost is what happens to the individual. This book grew from our desire to attend to the individual, to see the women.

Philosopher Marilyn Frye (1995) suggests women are not understood to be seers who count, to be witnesses who are believed. She develops a metaphor based on the idea of two people seeing the same statue, one from the front and one from the back. Both see the same statue, the same reality, but unless both are accepted as credible witnesses, one will be framed as mistaken about the nature of reality and one as correct (Frye 1995, 169–70). In American culture, she argues, women are the ones named as incredible. That seems to be the case in terms of birthing as well.

If you were to go to the maternity section in any large bookstore, you would find books authored by doctors, nurses, and people with "Ph.D." behind their names. In a search of popular media, including films, television, magazines, newspapers, and books, I found very few unmediated stories by women who had given birth (Sterk 1996). Instead, women's stories, if included at all, were mediated by the people culture has authorized to tell these stories. The stories may have been included in advice books authored by doctors, nurses, midwives, or scholars. Rarely did these stories take on a presence of their own. That is what I mean when I say the authors of this book see the women.

We have listened to the women themselves tell of their journey through birthing. In this book, we quote extensively from the interviews, giving those interviews a place of privilege in our work of making sense of giving birth. We partner with the women who told their stories. Our focus on the interviews allows us to bring women into the foreground of discussions about private decisions women may make about their own birthing choices and also into decisions on public policy affecting this important aspect of many women's lives and health. In this book, we do not orient our attention (as Frye would say) around fathers, medical personnel, or the baby. Instead, we orient it around women who have given birth and around their understandings of what birthing means.

The five authors of the chapters in this book share an understanding of women's experiences of giving birth as being culturally mediated, as well as directly experienced. The chapters show how women's actions and choices are circumscribed all around by assumptions of what birth means.

First, women rarely are allowed to tell stories of birthing. As Carla Hay and Krista Ratcliffe explain in chapters 1 and 2, stories of birth traditionally have been told, in sanitized and cleaned up versions, by historians, male novelists, and expert observers. Hay and Ratcliffe suggest that women are taught that it is rude to tell their own birthing stories; somehow, the stories are gross and disgusting, and telling them represents a breach of etiquette.

Second, we have found that women are subjected to an entire set of medically, legally, and economically legitimated protocols (common procedures) as soon as they enter a hospital. The amount of time women may labor before being prepared and ushered into a cesarean delivery, the number of days women may stay in the hospital, the amount of food and drink they may consume, and the kinds of pain support they may be offered are oriented around the idea that the birthing process should be controlled by standards of efficiency, rather than geared toward satisfactory care. In this book, Alice Kehoe, Leona VandeVusse, and I all give examples of ways in which control usurps care.

Third, we discovered that iatrogenic problems (ones caused by the hospital or the caregiver) often are framed as problems brought on by the women themselves. Carla Hay describes in chapter 1 how women were blamed for the puerperal fever that was caused by doctors' and nurses' inadequate attention to hygiene. On the basis of the charge that women were to blame for the infections, until recently, women routinely were subjected to pubic shaves, enemas, and antiseptic washes. Hay shows that medical rhetoric could not allow the idea to be broached that doctors could be causing the infections, since they were healers, not ones who made people sick. Later, in chapter 5, Leona VandeVusse explains how the use of electronic fetal monitoring, which has a high rate of false readings, has replaced listening to the fetal heart beat with a stethoscope. Based on the potentially faulty readings, decisions are being made about interventions such as forceps and cesarean delivery. Often the blame for incorrect readings by the machine is laid at women's feet: They moved too much or they allowed the monitor to slip.

Fourth, we found that birthing women are treated in ways all too similar to colonized peoples. In particular, Alice Kehoe develops this analogy in chapter 4. According to Sarah Hoagland, the mechanism of colonization operates by introducing a set of "values portraying the relationship of dominant colonizers to subordinate colonized as natural and normal" (Hoagland 1996, 177). Colonized peoples are framed as childlike, passive, in need of protection, and as desiring the domination of the colonizer (see, for example, Barry 1979; Morgan 1977). In order to keep colonized peoples in line, the colonizers prevent the colonized from learning and controlling key skills on their own. We have found this to be an apt description of the ways in which hospital-related caregivers treat women who are giving birth. This contrasts markedly from the ways in which midwifery's typical practices encourage women to be in tune with their own bodies. It is significant that the discourse and practices of midwifery are muted and marginalized in American culture, for these practices see the women by placing them in the foreground.

Given the hegemony of constraints on women's thought and experience, we found it illuminating that women think thoughts and do things they are not supposed to do. Some women hate pregnancy. Some do not follow a doctor's orders. Some avoid doctors entirely, giving birth in their homes, where they can control the experience. Some defy their caregivers, even if this is their own first birth. Some trust their bodies more than they do the experts. Most of all, however, women remember giving birth, in greater and more accurate detail than they "should."

Often, women facing birth are told they will forget the pain, they will forget the details of the birth once they hold the baby in their arms. Yet women don't forget. Even if they don't tell the stories often, they don't forget them. At ninety-five, the oldest woman interviewed (Nancy W.) still remembered vividly the pain she felt at being sewn up and the pleasure she took in her mother's presence at the birth of her babies. Her memory is not atypical. A longitudinal study completed by P. Simkin, in which she interviewed women shortly after they gave birth and then again twenty years later, found that women remembered a significant number of details of their birthing stories, and presented the stories in a similar organizational pattern and attitude even after all those years (Simkin 1991). These stories matter to women. For some women, the moment of giving birth defines who they are, while for others it is an important and necessary means to an end—the baby—and for still others it is a time of self-discovery. In any case, each birth is a unique event in the life of a woman. It may be just one more birth for the caregiver, but it may be the only birth for the mother, and its meaning often is filled with emotion and passion.

Based on what we discovered when we paid attention to the women, to seeing them see birth, we believe that significant policy changes are needed in the way birthing typically is conducted in America, particularly in the communication practices of caregivers. While the case for these changes will emerge from the five chapters of this book, just what those changes should be will be developed in the conclusion.

In chapter 1, historian Carla H. Hay sets the stage by explaining how birthing has been conducted in the United States. She shows that as time has gone on, women's bodies have come to be seen as machines. That metaphor encourages an assembly-line mentality on the part of hospital caregivers, a mentality that frames a perfect baby as the outcome of properly maintaining and manipulating a woman's body. As birthing practices have become more and more standardized and localized in hospitals, the baby has become the focus of attention. Given the goal of a perfect baby, the needs and desires of the mother have been placed at a lower priority.

In chapter 2, English scholar Krista Ratcliffe explores the loss to culture represented by women's public silence on childbirth. Comparing literary with lived narratives (drawn from the Birthing Project), Ratcliffe distinguishes between the qualities of re-presentation and presentation of birth. As birth often is represented, it happens in another room, bloodlessly. As presented by women who have done it, it is a presence, demanding attention by every fiber of one's being.

In the third chapter, I offer the stories of four women, progressing from a story of control by doctor-authorized protocols to one of self-directed home birth. I suggest there is a significant difference in women's satisfaction with birth when they feel cared for rather than controlled.

Alice Beck Kehoe, an anthropologist well versed in the lives and ways of Native Americans, raises the idea of colonization in chapter 4, arguing that the birthing practices performed on native populations rob them of their own ways and means of symbolizing and conducting birth. She places all women subjected to controlling practices on a continuum of colonization.

In chapter 5, Leona VandeVusse, director of a university midwifery program, analyzes women's responses to care they have received, showing that when women are involved in the decision making during labor and delivery, they are much happier about the experience. VandeVusse points the way toward alternatives for childbirth care that incorporate women as partners rather than patients in the process.

Finally, the conclusion draws on ideas developed in the five chapters and answers the question, "How, then, should birth be managed?" Given the ways in which birth has been framed, how women have complied with and resisted the framing, and how women have been affected by the framing, what might be better ways to facilitate good births? Taking its cue from VandeVusse's chapter, the conclusion will urge women to become more active participants in birthing, even when it takes place in the controlled setting of the hospital. Further, it will encourage public policy makers to find ways to respect the embodied experience of particular women giving birth. Doing so will honor the context of lifelong care and commitment in which many women labor, by treating them as partners.

Many people have helped in the creation of this book. We would like to thank them for their work. First and foremost, we thank the many women who agreed to be interviewed. We asked them to tell us about an experience filled with emotional, and even spiritual, meaning. For some it was an easy telling, for others, very difficult. We deeply appreciate their willingness to speak openly and at length.

Second come those who supported us in other ways. Marquette University, my academic home until recently, has provided the authors with four supportive and creative colleagues, all of whom found ways to incorporate thinking about childbirth into their lives. The five of us have spent many long hours together, wrangling over the point and direction of the book, coming to terms with the stories, and sharing our own stories. In addition, Marquette University's graduate school and College of Communication provided grant money to pay for much of the travel, taping, and transcribing needed to complete the Birthing Project, and, thus, this book. Calvin College played a key part in enabling the completion of the book by providing resources for research assistance and transcription services.

The authors of this book are indebted to the people who transcribed the interviews that form the database of this book, particularly Nancy Burns, Dawn Ksobiech, and Yvonne Posthuma. Without the transcriptions it would not have been possible to do the analysis, and the archive would not exist.

Research assistants have been at the elbows of most of the authors of this book. Their work made ours possible. In particular, I would like to thank Ellie White-Stevens for her organizational skills and Beverly Ryskamp for her categorizing expertise, as well as Margaret Wimp, for her support of Krista Ratcliffe through the editing process. Krista Ratcliffe thanks her husband, Kevin Brown, and her daughter, Olivia Ratcliffe Brown, for their love and inspiration.

Leona VandeVusse thanks her dear friends and colleagues who sustain, encourage, and challenge her daily—Gladys Simandl, Lisa Hason, and Kate Harrod—and her daughters, Alicia and Melissa, who teach and stretch her.

Without the faith of Michigan State University Press, this book would not be published. Many thanks go to our editor, Martha Bates, and to Martin Medhurst for recommending us to her.

Finally, I would like to thank my husband and children for affording me the experience of the rigors and excitement of giving birth. I only wish I could have read this book before I did it myself. My choices would have been quite different.

REFERENCES

Barry, K. 1979. Sex colonization. In *Female sexual slavery,* 163–204. Englewood Cliffs, N.J.: Prentice Hall.

Frye, M. 1995. To be and be seen: The politics of reality. In *Essential readings in theory: Reinterpretation and application,* ed. N. Tuana and R. Tong, 162–74 Boulder, Colo.: Westview Press.

Hoagland, S. 1996. Moral revolution: From antagonism to cooperation. In *Essential readings in theory: Reinterpretation and application,* ed. N. Tuana and R. Tong, 175–92. Boulder, Colo.: Westview Press.

Morgan, R. 1977. On women as a colonized people. In *Going too far: The personal chronicle of a feminist.* New York: Random House.

Nancy W. 1990. Interview by Helen Sterk, 26 August. Available from Memorial Library Archives, Marquette University, Milwaukee, WI 53201.

Simkin, P. 1991. Just another day in a woman's life: Women's long-term perceptions of their first birth experience. Part 1. *Birth* 18(4): 203–10.

Sterk, H. 1996. Contemporary birthing practices: Technology over humanity? In *Evaluating women's health messages: A resource book,* ed. R. L. Parrott and C. M. Condit, 124–34. Thousand Oaks, Calif.: Sage Publications.

1

CHILDBIRTH IN AMERICA
A Historical Perspective

Carla H. Hay

eproduction is essential to the survival of any species or culture. Only recently, however, have historians begun to focus on the reproductive rituals of humankind, heretofore the domain of anthropologists and sociologists. An escalating interest in social history that reflects the democratization of Western society and the influence of Marxist analysis, heightened by the impact of the 1970s feminist movement, has generated a massive outpouring of academic (and popular) studies of the "world we have lost" (Laslett 1965) and its technocratic replacement. Intensive scrutiny of both the intersection and the separation of public and private spheres has highlighted the often convoluted "sexual politics" of preindustrial and industrial society. Reproductive issues constitute a critical nexus between public and private domains.

The overweening importance of reproduction, as Crawford (1990) aptly observes, gives "all societies . . . an interest in controlling it." Indeed, "in no society known to us are women [in the aggregate] allowed to give birth however and whenever they choose" (3). Women's experience of birth is culturally mediated and consequently varies "enormously across time and space" (Marland and Rafferty 1997, 3). The physiological act of parturition is universal; not so "'the ways in which the process is experienced, endowed with meaning, and behaviorally managed'" (Michaelson 1988, 8). Whereas many non-Western societies view childbirth as a "function of health, rather than of illness," today most Americans "accept a biomedical model of birth . . . as a risk to be managed by the application of science and technology" (Michaelson 1988, 9). This was not always the "American way of birth" (Mitford 1992). Notwithstanding an element of peril inherent in pregnancy and childbirth, until relatively recently giving birth was considered a natural process which most women, irrespective of class and material circumstances, expected to experience several times during the span between puberty and menopause.

Prior to the twentieth century, science and technology had little or no impact on an event that was in some respects a social occasion. Most women were "brought to bed" in their homes in the company of female friends and a midwife, who was usually a woman. Reconstructing the historical process whereby this elemental human experience metamorphosed into a high-tech enterprise managed by highly trained specialists contextualizes late twentieth-century "birthing narratives" and provides perspective on the sometimes strident, often nostalgic contemporary discourse on childbirth.

Reconstructing the history of childbirth prior to the twentieth century is complicated by the fragmentary and unrepresentative character of the sources. The evidence is "biased towards the wealthy and the literate" (Crawford 1990, 14), whose diaries, correspondence, and, occasionally, published sentiments may be anomalous, even for their own class. The experiences of the underclass and minorities are often unknown, or are mediated through the perspective of the middle and upper classes. Much of the research to date on childbirth in colonial America, for example, focuses on populations culturally and biologically linked to the British Isles. Cultural variables that might differentiate the experience of settlers with ties to Holland, France, Sweden, Spain, Africa, or the Caribbean have received little attention. Racial and ethnic minorities are ill-defined characters in the historiography of childbirth in America. Moreover, reliance on easily accessible didactic medical and religious printed sources, largely male-authored, mutes female voices and risks metamorphosing the extraordinary into the typical, the prescriptive into reality. A tendency to focus on urban centers, where records are often more voluminous, distorts regional differences and glosses over the rural, agricultural culture that dominated the American and European landscape until the twentieth century. Finally, much of the historiography of childbirth has been characterized by a polemical tone. This is particularly evident in the frequently critical discussion of the physician's usurpation of the female midwife's role in childbirth. Leavitt (1996), for example, baldly states that "almost any intervention by the physician created a potential for harm" (238).

The culture of childbirth in colonial America reflected British and Continental traditions modified by the frontier environment. Fragmentary colonial data can be supplemented and contextualized by a judicious use of recently published studies of British and European birthing practices. The result is a more nuanced account of the American experience than would otherwise be feasible.

On an average, colonial women in British North America married at about age twenty-two and gave birth sixteen months later. Subsequent births occurred at fifteen- to twenty-month intervals until the mother was about forty years of age. In rural communities, until the nineteenth century, conception rates were highest in April, May, and June, declined rapidly from July through October, when harvesting crops consumed time and energy, picked up from November through January, a time of feasting and celebration, and declined again in February and March. With the exception of those white women in the southern colonies who utilized slaves as wet nurses, most women who were physically able to do so breast-fed their babies for at least one year. Colonial women were generally healthier and better nourished than their contemporaries in the Mother Country, with the consequence that their fertility rates were higher and the mortality rates for both mother and child were apparently lower than in Britain (Wertz and Wertz 1989). In some cases, frequent pregnancies undermined the mother's health and led to an early death, as was clearly the case with Thomas Jefferson's wife, Martha, who probably had several miscarriages in addition to delivering six children during her ten-year marriage. She never recovered from the birth of her last child in January 1782 and died in May of that year.

Determining if and when conception occurred was often difficult. (A reliable test was not available until the 1920s.) Professor James Blundell commented in 1834 that "the most certain mode of knowing whether a woman be in a state of gestation . . . is by waiting till the term of nine months is complete" (Oakley 1984, 17). In the colonial period there was even disagreement about the length of gestation, with some medical texts stipulating that the child could be born at seven months, although most believed nine and one-quarter months was normal. Female folk wisdom favored forty weeks (Pollock 1990, 44). Amenorrhea, or absence of the menses, followed by the quickening, were popular gauges of pregnancy. Prenatal care was minimal, although it was commonly believed until well into the nineteenth century that the fetus was "profoundly influenced by the mother's mental and emotional state" (Oakley 1984, 23). Women were encouraged to consume a "temperate" diet, avoiding "strong alcohol"(Pollock 1990, 50) and foods that might induce vomiting or constipation. Wine diluted with water was recommended. Vigorous exercise was discouraged, but most women engaged in their customary routines until shortly before their anticipated delivery. This continued to be the case for women on the American frontier well into the nineteenth century (King

1996). Any difficulties that developed during the pregnancy, other than those occasioned by an accidental injury, were usually attributed to an imbalance in the expectant mother's bodily fluids. Purgatives, blisters, leeches, and bleeding, which no less an authority than the eminent physician and philosopher John Locke said could be initiated at four months (Pollock 1990), were used to bring "bodily fluids and functions . . . into a more balanced state" (Oakley 1984, 16). Dr. John Clarke remarked in 1806 that "'bleeding from a large vein . . . will often be found extremely useful, and has much more effect in appeasing the sickness and vomiting of pregnant women, than any medicines taken into the stomach'" (Oakley 1984, 22). Reliance on bloodletting as a remedy for virtually any discomfort or distress experienced during the pregnancy or labor would not decline until after 1843, when Gabriel Audral discovered that the blood of pregnant women had a diminished number of red cells rather than an excess, as had previously been believed (Oakley 1984).

While the signal importance of reproduction to society meant men, particularly in rigidly patriarchal cultures, played a significant part in the definition of reproductive roles, rules, and rituals, it did not necessarily result in their active involvement in the delivery of the child. In early modern Western civilization, childbirth was, in fact, a social occasion controlled by females. Unless the mother lived some distance from her neighbors or gave birth unexpectedly or quickly, the birth would be a "public" event (Scholten 1985, 29), but the audience would be a small group of women, "gossips." The term is a "corruption of 'god-sib' or 'god-sibling,' that is someone invited to witness the birth for the subsequent purpose of the child's baptism" (Wilson 1995, 25). By the latter stages of her pregnancy, the expectant mother would have asked these women, who were friends, neighbors, and relations, including, oftentimes, her own mother, to support her during the delivery. The responsibility for assembling the coterie usually fell to the father-to-be. He would also help in the delivery if circumstances precluded gathering a female support group or if a particularly protracted and exhausting labor required his assistance as a surrogate birthing stool to hold his wife during contractions. Yet on most occasions he would absent himself from the "borning" or "birthing" room, frequently a small chamber behind the central chimney or the master bedroom in larger homes (Wertz and Wertz 1989). The gossips would use curtains and bits of cloth to envelop the area, shutting out light and drafts, metamorphosing the chamber into "a womb" (Gélis [1984] 1991, 97; Wilson 1990). They would also prepare food and drink for the mother, including toast, gruel, broth, eggs, and cordials or the cau-dle, a drink of ale or wine, mixed with sugar and spices. It was common-place in Europe for amulets to be placed strategically in the room and on the mother's person (Gélis [1984] 1991), and that custom may have been observed in the American colonies despite the opposition of religious authorities to practices that smacked of witchcraft and superstition. Even the noted seventeenth-century Puritan divine, Cotton Mather, recom-mended that a pregnant woman wear a lodestone which Mather believed functioned as a magnet holding the fetus in its mother's womb and less-ening the risk of miscarriage (Wertz and Wertz 1989).

In charge of the delivery itself was the midwife, the "with-woman," whom the mother had engaged some time before her confinement. In rural areas she might have had little discretion in her choice. On the other hand, the midwife in such communities would probably be a familiar and respected figure. Church and court records provide most of the fragmentary information available on colonial midwives. They often testified in infan-ticide and bastardy cases and served on "juries of matrons" who examined a felon who claimed to be pregnant ("pled her belly"), a circumstance that would stay her execution until three months after delivery. The rarity of a source such as the diary of Mrs. Martha Moore Ballard, a late-eighteenth-century midwife in Hollowell, Maine, who attended 996 deliveries, makes it difficult to generalize about the background, expertise, and techniques of colonial midwives. Studies critical of the medicalization of childbirth have tended to romanticize the midwife as a benign noninterventionist who encouraged the mother while patiently waiting for nature to take its course (Leavitt 1986). Recent scholarship, however, suggests that skill lev-els and techniques varied enormously (Wilson 1990, 74). Shorter (1982) differentiates between "highly qualified" urban midwives and their often impoverished, less professional rural counterparts who supposedly were "at a complete loss in dealing with any emergency" (36). This sweeping indict-ment is certainly not borne out by the record of Martha Ballard, whose career prompts Ulrich's (1996) equally problematic generalization that "rural midwives were capable of managing difficult as well as routine births" (229). More judiciously, Marland (1993) concludes that midwives "were not administering angels—they were ordinary working women, wage-earners, with a sense of pride in their occupation," and perhaps, "spe-cial qualities, of patience . . . and fellow-feeling" (8). They varied in age and marital status, but typically were married or widowed, mature, of "mid-dling" social rank, physically fit, and self-confident (Wilson 1995). Some learned their craft under the tutelage of another midwife; some drew on their own experiences in childbirth. Following the French example, formal training in a lying-in hospital became available on a limited basis for British midwives in the eighteenth century, facilitating their eventual recognition in the twentieth century as obstetrical professionals with primary responsibility for normal births (Forbes 1996; Oakley 1984). Efforts to initiate such training in postrevolutionary America were unsuccessful, a circumstance that contributed to the midwife's displacement by obstetricians in affluent urban households during the nineteenth century.

During the course of a normal delivery, some midwives contented themselves with keeping the mother warm, offering words of encouragement, and otherwise letting nature take its course. Other midwives massaged and applied lubricants to the abdomen, labia, and perineal tissue and stretched the labia to promote dilation and speed delivery. Laudanum and belladonna might be used to relieve the mother's pain. Gélis ([1984] 1991) notes that neither midwives nor physicians took any particular sanitary precautions until the late eighteenth century. During labor the mother assumed whatever birth posture regional custom and her own comfort dictated: crouching, kneeling, standing, sitting in another woman's lap or on the birth stool provided by the midwife (an adjustable version was styled the "'portable ladies' solace,'" Wertz and Wertz 1989, 13). Premature recourse to the stool could result in a prolapsed uterus. Not infrequently, midwives used scissors, a pin, or their fingernails to tear the amniotic membrane. As soon as some part of the child presented itself, they would then pull and manipulate it. (Gélis [1984] 1991; Wilson 1995). Some inserted their fingers or hand into the vagina to ascertain the progress of labor (Shorter 1982). Such techniques could, of course, result in lacerations of soft tissue or introduce infection resulting in puerperal fever. Concern that the neck of the womb would close before the placenta was naturally expelled prompted some midwives to attempt its manual extraction, a technique that could cause a prolapsed uterus, hemorrhaging ("flooding"), or the onset of puerperal fever, although cases of the latter were apparently infrequent (Ulrich 1996). Hemorrhaging, puerperal fever, or eclampsia (an acute phase of toxemia) were the most common causes of maternal mortality.

Difficult or obstructed births occurred in probably less than 5 percent of deliveries (Ulrich 1996). The rarity of their occurrence meant that most midwives would have had little experience with such crises (Wilson

1995). Techniques used to dislodge an obstructed fetus included inducing sneezing or vomiting. In Europe ergot was used to intensify uterine contractions and to expedite the expulsion of the placenta. It seems probable that some colonial midwives also used this drug, although Wertz and Wertz (1989) emphasize there is no evidence that they did so. It clearly was used in nineteenth-century America (Leavitt 1986). In the case of a breech presentation, some midwives might attempt to turn the child to the head (cephalic version), a technique requiring considerable skill that could only be performed early in labor. In other instances of malpresentation the child might be turned to the feet (podalic version), which could then be grasped to pull the child from its mother's body. If the birth came by the arm, the appendage might be cut off if the labor had been prolonged and there was consensus that the child was dead. The midwife might perform this procedure or a surgeon might be called in for this grisly task. Obstruction by the head could occur if the head was too large or was improperly rotated, if the mother's pelvis was too small or was malformed (often because of rickets, a dietary disorder that was more commonplace in Europe than the American colonies), or if the child's head was impacted because of inadequate dilation of the cervix or lubrication of the birth canal, possibly because of the premature rupturing of the amniotic sac by the midwife. After perhaps days of labor, and usually only if there was agreement that the child was dead or the mother's life was in jeopardy, a craniotomy would be performed on the child's skull with a crotchet, a hooklike device, and the child's body extracted, perhaps piecemeal. In an emergency, even fireplace hooks might be used in this procedure. In England, by the seventeenth century a surgeon was usually summoned for this gruesome operation. That might not have been feasible in many American communities, given the relative scarcity of physicians in the colonies prior to 1750. Although technically feasible, cesarean sections were almost never attempted, even to save a child after the mother had died (Wilson 1995; Shorter 1982). Consistently in crises the mother's life took primacy over the child's. Until the mid-eighteenth century, summoning the physician in a very real sense constituted the death knell of the child.

Such horrific conclusions to a woman's labor were rare. Instead, most deliveries were uncomplicated. After its umbilical cord was tied and cut, the infant was washed, swaddled, and shown to its mother. There followed a lying-in period of several days or weeks, depending upon the mother's economic circumstances and system of social support, during which she rested and recovered her strength. After being confined to bed for several days in a darkened room, she had her "upsitting," when the bed linen was changed and she received visits from her female relatives, friends, and neighbors. Usually male visitors were limited to relatives. A friend, relative, servant, or hired nurse looked after her household duties until the new mother felt able to resume these responsibilities herself. Wilson (1990) emphasizes that the effect of the lying-in was to withdraw from the husband, the patriarchal head of the household who ordinarily exercised jurisdiction over all family members, two of the most important and "customary fruits of marriage: his wife's physical labour and her sexual services" (87). Ironically, extended confinement in bed, which only the affluent could afford, was potentially perilous, since it could cause embolisms.

A woman's attitude toward her pregnancy and impending delivery has been at issue in much of the historiography on childbirth in early modern Western societies. Until recently, studies frequently characterized the experience as a time of peril for the mother and the child, a life-threatening but unavoidable episode (Sholten 1985; Leavitt 1986; Crawford 1990; Pollock 1990) that induced fear and anxiety and created a "collective sense of fearfulness" (Shorter 1982, 69). According to Porter and Porter (1988), childbirth "terrorized a mother's heart" (100), and Shorter (1982) asserts that "there is no doubt that the typical woman in the years before 1900 faced her approaching delivery with foreboding" (69). Leavitt (1986) concurs, maintaining that "women spent considerable time worrying and preparing for the *probability* [my italics] of not surviving their confinements" (20). According to Leavitt (1986), "fearful anticipation characterized the common and *realistic* [my italics] attitudes towards pregnancy" until the twentieth century (27). Leavitt (1986) goes so far as to argue that despite the low incidence of maternal mortality in the late twentieth century, pregnant women continue to "face their own mortality. . . . The centrality of childbearing to women's lives emphasizes the seriousness of the dangers it holds" (28).

Recent demographic studies have significantly revised previous assumptions about maternal mortality in childbirth. It now seems clear that in the seventeenth and eighteenth centuries the mother died in only about 1 percent of births (Wilson 1996), although inexplicably the rate was apparently as high as one in thirty births in early seventeenth-century Massachusetts (Shorter 1982). Confronted with such statistics, some historians, while acknowledging that women may have viewed death in childbirth as a rare event, nonetheless continue to emphasize the anxiety, indeed "dread," that childbearing could engender. Pollock asserts that "women rarely enjoyed the period of gestation, beset as they were with sickness, pain, and fear" (1990, 59). Crawford agrees with Mendelson that childbirth rituals served to reinforce the perception of birth as a time of agony and "terror" (Crawford 1990, 22). Even Wertz and Wertz (1989), whose reasoned history of childbirth in America is largely free of the hyperbole that detracts from some studies, generalize that "seventeenth-century women approached birth not with joy but with dread" (21). Much of the documentation for this mentality of fear, however, is derived from a "handful" of sources, prompting Wilson (1996) to conclude that, insofar as the British experience is concerned, the "direct evidence for the 'fear thesis' is unconvincing" (148). Her reservations are equally applicable to the American scene. Heavy reliance on New England sources, particularly sermons of seventeenth-century Puritan divines who characterized childbirth as a life-threatening time of travail (Leavitt 1986), may well distort the popular perception of the birth experience during the first century of colonial history. Indeed, women diarists in eighteenth-century America describe birth "matter-of-factly" rather than as an occasion of "dread" (Wertz and Wertz 1989, 24).

If, as Oakley (1984) observes, "we have no way of telling" if pregnant women were "more anxious in 1781 than in 1881 or 1981" (14), why do many historians continue to emphasize the traumatic potential of the event, since the "usual outcome was . . . 'a safe deliverance'" (Wilson 1995, 19)? Why insist, as does one of the standard histories of childbirth, that "during most of American history, an important part of women's experience of childbirth was their anticipation of dying or of being permanently injured during the event" (Leavitt 1986, 14)? Wilson (1996) suggests one explanation. The occasional "stark expressions of fear" (149) in primary sources stand out from otherwise prosaic chronicles, understandably captivating the historian. As Gélis ([1984] 1991) notes, "uneventful births had no history; they almost never held the attention of witnesses" (215). Once extrapolated from the original source, such "purple passages"(Wilson 1996, 149) are repeatedly cited as evidence of a cultural mind-set rather than interpreted as discrete expressions. Yet do other considerations explain why some historians of childbirth have so earnestly embraced the "fear thesis"? Depicting childbirth as a fearful and dangerous enterprise simultaneously enhances the stature and self-sacrifice and implies the victimization of legions of women who were obliged

by a patriarchal culture literally to put their lives at risk. Such a characterization serves to indict patriarchy while validating and valorizing otherwise unsung heroines. Framing childbirth in this fashion may say more
about the mind-set of some historians than the *mentalité* of birthing
women in the early modern period.

Interestingly, most accounts which focus on the pregnant woman's
supposed fear for her own well-being largely ignore a very real reason for
anxiety on her part before and during labor: the welfare of her child.
Infant mortality rates were certainly higher than those of maternal
deaths, although accurate statistics about miscarriages, stillbirths, and
infant deaths resulting from delivery are not available. In fact, concern for
the child proved a powerful motivation for enlisting the services of the
male surgeon, who had displaced the female midwife in the "birthing
rooms" of the upper classes by the early nineteenth century.

Science and technology dramatically affected the Western culture of
childbirth by introducing a male authority into a traditionally female
domain. More so than on the Continent, in England this development
marginalized female midwives. The circumstances and mind-set that
encouraged this critical shift in the dynamic of the English birthing room
warrant closer consideration, since Americans would mimic the English
model.

During the course of the seventeenth century, male surgeons in
England were involved with increasing frequency in difficult births. Their
services were sometimes booked prior to the onset of labor in cases where
the mother's anatomy (particularly a narrow pelvis) or previous birth
experiences indicated potential problems in labor. Much more frequently, they were summoned at a critical juncture during an obstructed
birth, usually to save a mother's life by surgically excising a presumably
dead infant from its mother's body. In either case, as Wilson (1995)
notes, "the surgeon's task was the delivery of a dead child in the tiny
minority of difficult births" (53). The "normal birth of a living child,"
which comprised the "vast majority of deliveries," was still the "province
of the midwife" (53). The forceps enabled the surgeon to breach the
domain of the midwife, to be summoned to the birthing room "not in
fear, but in hope" (Wilson 1996, 151), not to sacrifice a child to save a
mother, but to preserve the lives of both.

The forceps as well as the vectis (similar to the spoon occasionally
used by midwives to manipulate an obstructed fetus) and the fillet (flexi-
ble strips inserted in the uterus and looped around the child to extract it)

were invented by members of the Chamberlen family, who guarded the secret of these instruments, which enabled them to develop a lucrative practice as male midwives between 1620 and 1730. Early in the eighteenth century the instruments were sold, replicated, and publicized, generating a debate about their utilization that continued well into the nineteenth century. If used by an experienced practitioner, they could save an infant or ease a delivery after a protracted, often painful labor. If used prematurely or inexpertly, they could lacerate or maim both mother and child. Nonetheless, these instruments so quickly advantaged the surgeon at the midwife's professional expense that the failure of most midwives to include these new tools in their own repertoire is perplexing. Since most deliveries were normal and did not require extraordinary intervention, many midwives may have concluded that investing in the instruments was not worthwhile. Moreover, during this time period the forceps were often used before the fetal head was low in the birth canal, a procedure requiring considerable physical strength. Most telling, however, may have been the "simple force of custom which associated men with instrumental interference " (Wertz and Wertz 1989, 39).

The availability of the new instruments coincided with the publication of several medical texts reflecting a Cartesian view of the body as a machine. Particularly significant were François Mauriceau's *The Accomplisht Midwife* (1668); Hendrik van Deventer's account (1701) of the size, shape, and obstetric significance of the female pelvis; Fielding Ould's discussion of the rotation of the fetal head in labor (1742); William Smellie's published lectures on midwifery (1742) and *Treatise on the Theory and Practice of Midwifery* (1752), which provided the first precise measurements of the female pelvis and promoted the use of the forceps; and William Hunter's *Anatomy of the Human Gravid Uterus* (1774), which explained the function of the placenta. These studies significantly enhanced the understanding of female anatomy and the various stages of childbirth. Theoretical knowledge was augmented by clinical observation of childbirth in lying-in hospitals established for poor women during the eighteenth century. Armed with a supposedly superior scientific education and life-saving instruments, the male physician was positioned to challenge the midwife's primacy in normal deliveries.

At the beginning of the eighteenth century, male physicians seldom participated in normal deliveries in England. By the 1770s the "hegemony" of midwives was "fractured" and male physicians dominated the prestigious and "lucrative" delivery of the children of aristocratic and

wealthy women (Wilson 1995, 166, 169). The male physician's usurpation of the traditional midwife's role in normal births provoked occasional but ultimately ineffectual protests that emphasized the
impropriety of men breeching the privacy of the birthing room, "'a manifest violation of modesty, and the scandal of all good people'" (Wilson
1995, 167). By the nineteenth century, English "midwives were mostly
women of little education and generally no social status; their patients
were the same" (Schnorrenberg 1996, 157).

The male midwife's success was predicated in part on an increasingly
pejorative characterization of female midwives and traditional childbirth
rituals. As Dr. John Grigg observed in his 1789 *Advice to the Female Sex in
General, Particularly those in a State of Pregnancy and Lying-in:*

> It is much to be regretted, that there are yet many of the [female] sex, who
> are prejudiced in favour of ancient, erroneous opinions and customs, and
> thereby exclude themselves from the advantages they might reap by consult-
> ing those who are better acquainted with the human frame, and have
> acquired a much greater share of this species of knowledge, than others can
> with any reason be supposed to be in possession of. (Oakley 1984, 13)

In addition to denigrating his traditional female competition and
promoting his own superior education, the male midwife also assidu-
ously cultivated a bedside manner that would endear him to genteel
women, whose endorsement could insure the growth of both his obstetrical and his general practice. In the words of the eminently successful
London practitioner, William Hunter,

> In all degrees of midwifery the accoucheur's behavior should be conducted
> in such a manner as not to merit the calumnious censure of the family
> through precipitation [i.e., precipitate action] or temerity. A proper degree of
> seeming tenderness and sympathy can never do a man any disservice but
> often the contrary. (Wilson 1995, 176)

In an "age of reason," the professional credentials of the male midwife
particularly appealed to the "enlightened" upper classes. Wilson (1995)
persuasively argues that a new female culture was emerging in the eighteenth century, characterized by "literacy and leisure" (187). The "traditional role of the midwife was embedded in the collective culture of
women" (185). Childbirth had been the great social leveler, exposing the

"aristocratic lady and the cottager's wife to the same risks of illness and even death" (191). The pain of childbirth cruelly confounded the concept of "gentle birth" (191). The midwife served as a "tangible reminder that ladies were mere women" (191). Wilson suggests that the employment of male midwives reflected the fracturing of female culture in the eighteenth century and was one way for aristocratic and upwardly mobile bourgeois women to distinguish themselves from their social and economic inferiors. Affording the "exclusive fees" and technical services of the male midwife enabled affluent and genteel women to distance themselves from their inferiors and the "dangers of childbirth" (191). Male midwifery reflected the "new culture of class" and was an expression of "conspicuous consumption" (191). Affluence and urbanization were widening the divide between social classes in the eighteenth century. The educated male midwife was a manifestation of the growing gulf between an increasingly consumer-oriented, literate, affluent, urban social order and a rural folk culture grounded in oral tradition. In utilizing the male midwife's services, the genteel literate lady embraced that new cultural ethos and distanced herself from "the traditional, oral, collective culture—once the collective culture of all women, [but] now that of the lower" classes (187). Yet doing so entailed a "new form of dependence upon men" (187). On the other hand, at a time when the differentiation between the private and the public domain was intensifying, the presence of the male midwife in the birthing room served as a link between the domestic world of women and the professional world of men. Wertz (1996) puts a psychological spin on the phenomenon, suggesting women may have chosen male midwives because they wanted a male witness to their suffering, presumably to validate their painful contribution to the family's future prosperity. In that same vein, the male midwife may have served as a surrogate for the spouse at a time when there is clear evidence of growing emphasis on affection as a bond in marriages. Finally, the idealization of the "companionate marriage" (Stone 1977, 325) coincided with heightened attention to the development and well-being of children, given compelling expression in Lockean epistemology and the influential educational tracts of Jean Jacques Rousseau. In the course of the eighteenth century, the male midwife came to be perceived by elites as best able to promote the interests of both the infant and its mother.

These dramatic changes in the English pattern of childbirth were replicated in America, albeit at a somewhat slower pace for a variety of reasons, including the absence of a metropolitan market on the scale of

London to launch male midwifery, and the disruptive impact of the revolutionary war. Prior to 1750 there were relatively few physicians and no
medical schools or hospitals in the colonies. Thereafter the numbers of
physicians in America increased significantly. Many were trained in the
British Isles, bringing the expertise, technologies, and attitudes of the Old
World to the New. The Medical College of Philadelphia was founded in
1765, King's College (Columbia) Medical School in 1767, and Harvard
in 1782. Obstetrics was the first specialty taught in these schools,
although practitioners were not styled obstetricians until 1828, when the
term (from the Latin meaning to stand before) was coined as an alternative to man-midwife, a phrase that had always discomfited because of its
unprofessional, gendered association (Wertz and Wertz 1989). The field
could be quite lucrative. Because of the time invested in attending a
woman in labor, delivery fees were higher than fees charged for other
"routine" services, and a satisfied patient would often engage the physician for other medical treatment as well as recommending him to friends
and acquaintances (Wertz 1996).

Initially, as had been the case with some British practitioners,
American doctors envisioned midwifery as an "enterprise to be shared
between themselves and trained midwives"(Wertz and Wertz 1989, 44),
who would be responsible for the more tedious and time-consuming
aspects of labor. Dr. Valentin Seaman in New York City and Dr. William
Shippen in Philadelphia began teaching courses in anatomy and midwifery. Shippen's curriculum included clinical observation of births. Few
women enrolled in the classes, however, and efforts to organize practicing midwives into associations that might have enhanced their professional standing were unsuccessful. Wertz and Wertz (1989) attribute the
failure of these initiatives to "the tradition of local self-help empiricism
that continued to be very strong in America" (46). Yet the midwives' resistance to new modes of learning and of practicing their craft is paradoxical, since the country was peopled by individuals who were willing to
sever traditional spatial ties and who were in the process of creating a new
political system that constituted a marked departure from traditional as
well as contemporary structures. By distancing themselves from the new
learning and eschewing professional organizations, midwives themselves
facilitated their marginalization in the changing world of obstetrics.
Although midwives continued to minister to immigrants and the poor in
urban areas and were widely employed in rural communities until the
twentieth century, they were displaced by their male counterparts in the

birthing rooms of affluent and middle-class urban women by the early nineteenth century. Whereas the 1815 Philadelphia City Directory listed twenty-one female and twenty-three male midwives, the 1819 directory listed only thirteen female, but forty-two male midwives. By 1824 there were only six female midwives (Scholten 1985).

Although revolutionary and early republican America was less bound by tradition than Europe, urban elites proved particularly receptive to the new scientific medicine embodied in the male midwife. In a newly con-stituted republic soon to mandate primary education for its citizens, edu-cational credentials carried considerable weight. As in England, the vaunted expertise of the male physician was a significant factor in his appeal to genteel American women. The contention that "'the well instructed physician is best calculated to avert danger and surmount diffi-culties'" (Scholten 1985, 37) withstood the argument that "'True Modesty is incompatible with the Idea of employing a MAN-MIDWIFE'" (Wertz and Wertz 1989, 56). Even lurid assertions that male midwives, "'inflamed with the thoughts of [the] well-shaped bodies of the women they have delivered, handled, hung over for hours,'" would take advantage of their vulnerable patients, driving them to "'adultery and madness'" (Wertz and Wertz 1989, 97), did not impede the growing popularity of the male mid-wife in elite circles.

The rationale that the male midwife could better serve the interests of the child as well as the mother was also persuasive in the new republic, where the eighteenth-century focus on the child was exalted in the con-cept of "Republican Motherhood" (Kerber 1980, 11). Abigail Adams had asked the Founding Fathers to "remember the ladies" (Kerber 1980, 82) when constituting the new nation. Instead of receiving political and legal rights, however, female patriots, whose wartime efforts had been instru-mental in victory over the Mother Country, were exhorted to focus on their domestic responsibilities of giving birth and inculcating civic virtue in the next generation of American citizens. The concept of "Republican Motherhood" underscored the importance of the child to the new nation's future prosperity and provided another incentive for patriotic women to engage the services of a male midwife, whose expertise and technological skill seemed to offer greater assurance of a "safe delivery" than the folk wisdom of the midwife.

"Republican Motherhood" also ennobled a "cult of domesticity" that flourished in America during the nineteenth century as urbanization and industrialization further widened the divide between private and public spheres. The cult extolled the "hand that rocks the cradle," reinforcing the imperative that both mother and child should flourish. The cult also glorified the leisured lady. Employment, even as a midwife, was increasingly perceived as unsuitable for ladies. Published in 1808, the *Married Lady's Companion and Poor Man's Friend*, an early childbirth manual, not only questioned the competence of female midwives but argued that they had "overreached their proper position in life." No "'true' woman would want to gain the knowledge and skills necessary" (Wertz and Wertz 1989, 56) to be a midwife. An 1820 Boston pamphlet, presumably penned by a respected obstetrician, boldly asserted that women "have not that power of action, or that active power of mind, which is essential to the practice of a surgeon. They have less power of restraining and governing the natural tendencies to sympathy and are more disposed to yield to the expressions of acute sensibility" (Wertz and Wertz 1989, 57). As the cult of domesticity pervaded middle-class households, midwifery became an occupation dominated by working-class women and gentlemen (Wertz and Wertz 1989). Consequently, despite the greater egalitarianism of the American republic, genteel American ladies would mimic their English counterparts by choosing a physician, a gentleman, to attend them in childbirth rather than an ill-educated working-class woman.

Although the male midwife displaced his female counterpart in the birthing rooms of the middle and upper classes, the traditional rituals of lying-in persisted until the late nineteenth century, with several class-based modifications reflecting the cult of domesticity, which emphasized the refined sensibilities of the fairer sex. When respectable women could no longer disguise their "delicate condition," they were expected to minimize public appearances during their confinement, something urban and rural working women could not do. Furthermore, beginning in the late eighteenth century in affluent households which could afford the expense of soiled bed linens, delivery moved to the bed from the floor or the birthing stool, which was "'uncomfortable, looked repellent, and put women in a panic . . . [as] an ominous symbol of pain in birth'" (Shorter 1982, 145).

Women in the Victorian era continued to orchestrate events in the "birthing" room (Leavitt 1986; Stowe 1996), but many physicians must have resented a gaggle of females questioning or even overriding recommended procedures. During labor, a physician often found himself pressured by his patient's friends and relatives to intervene in the process. Resisting demands for "'speedy relief'" (Shorter 1982, 155), even if acquiescing could be counterproductive or dangerous, might jeopardize the doctor's prospect for references and future business. As one physician remarked, "Perhaps the best way to manage normal labor is to let it alone, but you cannot hold down a job and do that" (Leavitt 1986, 61). In the latter half of the nineteenth century, the "place and role of physicians in birthing rooms across America" was "enhanced" (Leavitt 1986, 122) by the introduction of new anesthetics. Yet this significant innovation in the culture of childbirth also increased the potential for disagreement between physician and client.

Chloroform was first used in a delivery in 1847 by Dr. James Simpson of Edinburgh. Many obstetricians, apprehensive about the effects of anesthesia on the laboring mother and unborn child, were reluctant to follow Simpson's example. By contrast, their patients usually welcomed the alleviation of pain during delivery. In her study of childbirth regimens among the nineteenth-century British aristocracy, Lewis (1986) emphasizes cultural shifts in the perception of pain. Once again, class bias factored into changing attitudes and actions. Previously the pain of childbirth was perceived, even sanctified, as the inevitable price paid by the daughters of Eve, irrespective of social status, for fulfilling the biblical mandate to "be fruitful and multiply." In an increasingly secular, industrial age engaged in inventing machines to defy the limitations of the natural universe, the argument that the pain of childbirth was inevitable was no longer persuasive. If nature could be defied in other ways, why should women, especially women of quality, be debased, reduced to the state of moaning, writhing animals by needless suffering? Thomas Carlyle's contention that women should "patiently undergo all misery" (Lewis 1986, 231) was an attitude rejected by many women of privilege who instead shared Queen Victoria's enthusiasm for that "'blessed chloroform'" (Weintraub 1987, 224). The queen described the effect of the anesthetic, which she was given in 1853 during the delivery of her eighth child, as "soothing, quieting and delightful beyond measure" (Weintraub 1987, 224). As Lewis (1986) observes, traditional culture's identification of womanhood with the "passive endurance of pain and . . . agony was essentially masochistic, suiting a society in which women occupied a subordinate place and in which endurance was hailed as the prime female virtue (231). Wertz and Wertz (1989) suggest that "many women sought a painless birth as a sign of their . . . release from feminine roles that made them weak and dependent" (115). The sentimental focus on female delicacy that characterized the cult of domesticity or "true womanhood" promoted the increasingly prevalent conviction that "civilized and refined" women could not and should not tolerate such degradation. The converse of this logic was the widespread unsubstantiated belief that Native American, African American, and working-class women did not suffer in childbirth to the same degree as genteel women (Wertz and Wertz 1989; Scholten 1985; Leavitt 1986). The latter's heightened sensibilities, together with an indolent lifestyle and constrictive attire, which could deform their rib cages, supposedly rendered them particularly susceptible to the pangs of childbirth. The degree to which this construction of pain "was real, imagined, or simulated experience" (Wertz and Wertz 1989, 113) cannot be ascertained. Wertz and Wertz maintain that primarily because of concerns about "the necessity and the safety of anesthesia," most American doctors used such medication "infrequently" (1989, 117) in the latter half of the nineteenth century. Leavitt (1986), however, argues that women demanded this "panacea," described in 1847 by its first American beneficiary, Fanny Longfellow, as the "greatest blessing of this age" (122, 115). According to Leavitt, many physicians, despite their earlier reservations, "adopted anesthesia generally" (122) in the late nineteenth century.

The apparent discrepancy between the Wertz and Leavitt studies may be partially attributable to the fact that most physicians did not document their cases in sufficient detail for historians to determine conclusively the techniques and technologies regularly utilized by doctors. Ascertaining the consonance between medical texts and actual behaviors in the birthing room is particularly problematic. Prescriptive literature, for example, exhorted physicians to safeguard female modesty by refraining from pelvic exams. Although the vaginal speculum was invented in France in 1801, as late as 1851 the American Medical Association discouraged its use on the grounds it offended women and was thus "hazardous for the doctor's reputation and status" (Wertz and Wertz 1989, 90). According to medical texts, delivery should be cloaked by a woman's garments and bedding, even if forceps were used. A common technique during labor to minimize embarrassment for patient and physician was for the woman to lie on her side, facing away from the doctor. But both Wilson (1995) and Lewis (1986) contend that British women were not unwilling to be examined by their male physicians if circumstances warranted. They conclude that modesty concerned the doctor more than the patient. Perhaps, as Wertz and Wertz (1989, 78) assert, the "wave of prudery" that "engulfed" America in the early nineteenth century made American women more reluctant than their English counterparts to be examined by male doctors. Stowe's study (1996) of obstetrics in the American South suggests otherwise. Based on his analysis of the daybooks, letters, and diaries of physicians practicing in the antebellum South, Stowe concludes that "modesty did not survive the realities of labor and delivery" (319).

Stowe also highlights significant regional variations in the culture of childbirth in nineteenth-century America. Southern physicians often took a paternalistic attitude toward slave women, but were contemptuous toward poor white women. By contrast, in the urban teaching hospitals of the North and Midwest poor women potentially benefited from treatment by "some of the finest obstetricians" (Leavitt 1986, 75) in the nation. Yet these women also served as guinea pigs, providing "hands on" clinical experience for medical students. Ironically, obstetricians whose training did not include a clinical component received their "hands on" experience from their respectable patients, on whom they practiced, literally.

Although training in maternity hospitals that served poor and unmarried women provided valuable experience for practitioners of "scientific medicine" (Wertz and Wertz 1989, 136), it also encouraged a tendency to focus on the difficult delivery. The frequency of traumatic births in these facilities undoubtedly exceeded that found in the general population, given the poor nutrition and unsanitary and arduous lifestyle of many of the patients. Moreover, these institutions were breeding grounds for deadly puerperal fever. That physicians teaching or trained in this environment might be predisposed to see every birth as a "potential disaster," each woman as a "potential victim" (Wertz and Wertz 1989, 136, 128) is understandable. The consequence was a redefinition of pregnancy in the course of the twentieth century as a "potentially pathological" (Oakley 1984, 2) condition that requires careful monitoring and management, particularly during delivery. Labor came to be viewed as a "mechanical process that takes place in a machine inherently predisposed to malfunction" (Davis-Floyd 1988, 159), a modern variant on the Aristotelian perception of females as defective beings. Women were seen as "at risk by virtue of their embodiment as women" (Oakley 1992, 268). Dr. Henry Newman articulated this perspective in 1893, characterizing the "normal process of reproduction . . . [as] a formidable menace to the after-health of the parous woman" (Leavitt 1986, 29). Dr. Joseph DeLee of Chicago, in his day the "most influential [American] exponent of . . . [prophylactic] interventions in normal births" (Wertz and Wertz 1989, 141), believed that "'only a small minority of women' escaped damage" and many babies were killed or injured as a consequence of the natural process of labor, leading him to wonder if "Nature did not deliberately intend women to be used up in the process of reproduction, in a manner analogous to that of the salmon, which dies after spawning" (Wertz and Wertz 1989, 143). DeLee's use of outlet forceps and episiotomy to preclude serious injury to the mother and child during labor became routine hospital procedure during the 1930s.

In a very real sense the "worst case" scenario approach to childbirth by modern medicine echoes the exaggerated dread with which early modern women supposedly approached delivery. Interestingly, some of the same scholars (Leavitt 1986; Wertz and Wertz 1989) who sympathetically argue that yesteryear's mothers understandably feared childbirth because it was occasionally fatal fault modern physicians for predicating an interventionist approach to obstetrical treatment on the possibility something might go awry.

Ironically, many of the physician-initiated interventions in childbirth that were routinized in the late nineteenth and early twentieth century were the consequence of efforts to combat puerperal fever. This frequently fatal illness is a "classic example of iatrogenic disease—that is, disease caused by medical treatment itself" (Wertz and Wertz 1989, 128). Dr. Oliver Wendell Holmes speculated as early as 1843 that puerperal fever was a "contagion" spread by doctors, a contention fiercely resisted by many members of his profession as "incompatible" with the physician's role as "comforter" and "'minister of mercy'" (Wertz and Wertz 1989, 120–21). Louis Pasteur identified the streptococci cause of the fever around 1880. Since antiseptics were not systematically used, however, despite Joseph Lister's 1867 essay on surgical antisepsis, and because the traumatic interventions that could occasion infection increased in ensuing years, puerperal fever continued to be a deadly problem in both home and hospital deliveries until the 1940s, when sulfa and penicillin offered successful treatments of the infection. In the interim, the efforts of medical personnel to prevent puerperal fever contributed to the "dehumanization of birth" (Wertz and Wertz 1989, 128) by standardizing obstetrical procedures as part of an attempt to create a "germ-free environment" (Leavitt 1986, 161). Initially imposed on charity patients whose hygienic habits may well have been problematic, the new regimen included mandatory bathing, donning a hospital gown, shaving or clipping pubic hair that might harbor infectious agents, and using an enema to eliminate fecal contamination and a vaginal douche of saline and bichloride of mercury before and after delivery. Concern for asepsis also encouraged recourse in the 1930s to the lithotomy position for delivery. Increasingly, doctors were convinced that it was impossible to achieve an antiseptic environment in private homes—indeed, efforts to do so were frequently resisted by the mother's entourage. Birthing rooms were often cramped and, particularly in the domiciles of the poor, even fetid and visibly dirty. Moreover, the lighting in private dwellings contrasted unfavorably with that of the hospital, where trained staff (as distinct from meddlesome, perhaps emotional nonprofessionals) were available to assist the doctor as conditions warranted. Given these circumstances, doctors promoted hospitalization for the delivery of even their genteel patients despite the potential for contagion at such facilities.

In important respects the hospital would be a "great leveler" (Leavitt 1986, 82), mandating various preparatory procedures for women irrespective of their socioeconomic backgrounds. Nonetheless, class would continue to differentiate birth experience. The affluent were sequestered in private or semi-private rooms instead of being bedded in wards. Moreover, cultural stereotypes persisted within this ostensibly impersonal space and impacted on treatment. Not infrequently, for example, the tradition that women from certain social and ethnic groups "made more noise but suffered less pain and . . . needed less analgesia or anesthesia" (Wertz and Wertz 1989, 169) resulted in the insufficient medication of minority and poor women.

Many physicians may have favored the hospital as terrain that would significantly enhance their control of both process and patient (Leavitt 1986). Yet Shorter (1982) suggests that expectant mothers and doctors shared an even more important motivation in favoring the hospital over the home. At the hospital the most up-to-date technologies and techniques could be utilized to protect the health of the mother and her infant. cesareans required hospitalization, and innovative devices such as X-ray equipment simply could not be transported to the home. The hospital was the most efficient space in which to deliver, and in America efficiency was a watchword of the twentieth century. The twentieth-century hospital came to be perceived by both doctor and client as offering the best opportunity for a "safe delivery" (Shorter 1982, 160). Prior to 1900 less than 5 percent of women delivered in hospitals, which were identified with the indigent, the immoral, and the diseased. By 1939 50 percent of all women and 75 percent of all urban women delivered in hospitals. By the 1960s virtually all deliveries took place in a hospital. In the process, midwives, who still presided over about 50 percent of deliveries in 1900, virtually disappeared from the ranks of birth attendants in America. In England, by contrast, a history of professional organization and formal training enabled midwives to assume responsibility in the twentieth century for most "normal" births in government-regulated medical programs (Tew 1990). Ultimately, moreover, the increasing reliance on anesthesia and recourse to specialized surgical procedures, particularly cesareans, would force the general practitioner out of the delivery room, which became the domain of the obstetrical specialist. By 1986, in keeping with a widespread trend toward specialization in many professions, almost 90 percent of all deliveries in the United States were attended by specialists.

The dramatic shift from home to hospital reflected and furthered significant changes in the experience and rituals of childbirth that mirrored cultural shifts in industrial America. In the twentieth century childbirth ceased to be a "collective event" (Wilson 1995, 204) as female networks fragmented. Accelerating urbanization, increased mobility, the work rhythms of industry and commerce, the growing emotional bonding between spouses that distanced friends and relatives from the nuclear family, as well as changing attitudes toward privacy eroded the underpinnings of the traditional "lying-in." Women of various social classes found it increasingly difficult to gather a coterie of attendants who would support them in childbirth, despite the fact that decreasing fertility rates over the course of the century heightened the significance of each pregnancy, the value of each infant. In addition, the decline in immigration and increase in public sector employment after World War I substantially reduced the pool of domestic help for hire. These fundamental social and economic changes facilitated moving childbirth from the home to the hospital, a development that many women welcomed.

Shifting the site of childbirth from a decidedly private space to an institutional public space was also a manifestation of the increasingly widespread movement of twentieth-century American women into the public preserves of men. Challenging the cult of domesticity, over the course of the century the "new woman" secured the vote, accessed the university, and entered the industrial and white-collar labor force in record numbers. The introduction of maternity clothes in 1904 symbolized this "new" twentieth-century woman's rejection of the nineteenth-century culture of confinement. The new garments were marketed as enabling a woman to "live normally . . . to go about among other people." Rather than being "shut-in . . . hiding in darkness and gloom," embarrassed by "false modesty," the expectant mother could be "carefree . . . in the . . . sunshine . . . where . . . every day is a day of joy" (Wertz and Wertz 1989, 148–49). Delivery at the hospital "became normative . . . because women . . . had aspirations, . . . which the hospital seemed able to fill" (Wertz and Wertz 1989, 148).

For many women the hospital provided a refuge and respite from their domestic responsibilities. To attract clientele to hospitals early in the twentieth century, efforts were made to produce "charming effects" that rendered hospitals "rather quiet places in which to rest" (Wertz and Wertz 1989, 157). One mother rhapsodized that "the prospect of two weeks in that heavenly place tempted me to stay pregnant all the rest of my life" (Leavitt 1986, 171). Although the late-twentieth-century hospital projects an institutional image that few would characterize as celestial, many mothers still appreciate the brief relief it provides from other responsibilities.

As America transitioned from the age of Victoria to the era of the flapper, the hospital was also touted as the venue in which women could at long last "tame the birth experience" (Shorter 1982, 159). The cultural ethos of the country was grounded in an ongoing struggle to master and exploit nature, a powerful and enduring motif that infuses the development and ready adoption of a long list of techniques and technologies that seem to empower the laboring mother by promising a degree of control over a natural process. Early in the twentieth century this aspiration energized a militant campaign by a small cadre of upper- and middle-class women, many of them suffragists, to make "twilight sleep" available in the United States. Developed in Germany, the technique, which required hospitalization, entailed injecting women with morphine at the beginning of labor, followed by a dose of scopolamine. An amnesiac, this drug eliminated all memory of the delivery, however traumatic it might have been. Described by its proponents as "the greatest boon the Twentieth Century could give to women" (Leavitt 1986, 128), the procedure was initially resisted by doctors, who worried, as had chloroform's critics, about pernicious side effects for mother and child. Launching an intense lobbying effort in 1914, women advocates of "twilight sleep" overcame medical resistance to its use. Although the treatment remained controversial, by 1938 it was used in all Boston hospital deliveries (Wertz and Wertz 1989). The paradox of women fiercely agitating for their sex's right to choose the oblivion of "twilight sleep" (Leavitt 1986) highlights the ongoing interest of women in achieving relief from labor's pain. By the 1930s both "public and medical opinion agreed that 'some form of narcotization'" (Leavitt 1986, 140) should be used during childbirth. Eventually, spinal anesthesia and epidurals provided seemingly safe alternatives to drugs like scopolamine.

Accelerating or inducing labor to minimize maternal trauma and discomfort has a long history dating back to the heyday of the midwife. By the 1920s induction occurred in approximately 9 percent of births. One father observed, "the old way [of having a baby] was no fun." He much preferred the "new way—the easy, painless, streamlined way" (Leavitt 1986, 180). He and his wife had attended a matinee, dined, and then gone to the hospital at the appointed hour, previously agreed upon with her doctor. Following delivery, the mother enthused: "Why, I wouldn't mind having another baby next week . . . if that's all there is to it" (Leavitt 1986, 180). This couple's delighted response to induction was shared by Dr. James Voorhees, who commented in 1917, "Nothing pleases me more in my obstetrical work than to have a baby born a week or two ahead of time. . . . Consequently it is not unusual for me to try to 'shake the apple off the tree' ahead of time by castor oil and quinine" (Shorter 1982, 165). Voorhees believed that woman could more easily deliver small babies. To achieve this goal, in addition to induction, he recommended reducing carbohydrates in the expectant mother's diet after the sixth month. Minimizing weight gain was also promoted by physicians as a method to prevent eclampsia.

Accelerating or inducing labor could also enhance the birth experience for hospital personnel. Doctors had never relished the tedium and vocalization that typified birthing, and often gladly allowed others—midwives, the mother's coterie—to support a woman during the earlier stages of labor. Not surprisingly, in responding to the influx of patients as the hospital became the preferred site for delivery, the institution favored procedures that seemed most efficient and expeditious, and least disruptive of the facility's overall management. Routines were developed that sometimes better served the hospital's administrative needs and the professional (and personal) interests of medical personnel than the aspirations of the expectant mother, who was only a temporary visitor (Wertz and Wertz 1989). As with the customs of the traditional lying-in, hospital rituals could provide stability and reassurance for both the mother and her hospital attendants at a stress-inducing time. Yet they could also reinforce the mother's sense of vulnerability and dependence on the institution. The use of wheelchairs, for example, suggests the mother is disabled by her condition. Intravenous drips are her "umbilical cords to the hospital" (Davis-Floyd 1992, 95).

By World War II the assembly line had become the "metaphor for hospital birth" (Davis-Floyd 1996, 252), a decidedly "mixed" metaphor. When first developed by Henry Ford, the assembly line promised efficiency, productivity, and prosperity. Automation continues to have these advantages, but it can also jeopardize jobs and produce an impersonal and inhumane environment. Wertz and Wertz (1989) suggest that women may have initially welcomed a mechanistic model of childbirth. Historically "burdened with social and moral expectations about birth" (159), the "body as machine" analogy could relieve expectant mothers of a degree of personal responsibility should the "machine" malfunction. Moreover, as with the imagery of the assembly line, the machine as entity and metaphor had positive connotations, both epitomizing and symbolizing human mastery over nature. On the other hand, within Western culture there is also a tradition of ambivalence about the "machine in the garden" (Marx 1964). The machine can pollute, deface, and destroy the beauty and wonder of nature. As the "charming" hospital space of the 1920s evolved into the sterile, impersonal, and sometimes inhumane institution of later years (Michaelson 1988), criticism of the "technocratic model" (Davis-Floyd 1996) escalated.

The "consensus" (Wertz and Wertz 1989, 167) about the medicalization of childbirth began to break down at a point in time when modern medicine had rendered childbirth safer for the mother than ever before. By the 1950s, drugs, antibiotics, blood banks, new transfusion techniques, clotting agents, and surgical procedures such as cesareans had virtually eliminated or effectively responded to the historic causes of maternal mortality—fetal obstruction, puerperal fever, hemorrhaging, and eclampsia. Once maternal mortality ceased to be a pressing concern, attention could and did shift to other aspects of the birth experience.

Two of the most vocal critics of the hospital-based ritual of childbirth were themselves physicians: British obstetrician Dr. Grantly Dick-Read, whose *Childbirth without Fear* was published in the United States in 1944, and Dr. Ferdinand Lamaze, whose Pavlovian childbirth technique was popularized by Marjorie Karmel in *Thank You, Dr. Lamaze*, published in 1959. In common they advocated minimizing medical intervention, particularly the use of anesthesia, to enhance the mother's birth experience.

Just as the initial embrace of the technocratic model of childbirth reflected broader cultural currents, so also the emerging critique of that

paradigm was a manifestation of sometimes paradoxical trends in the latter half of the twentieth century. The "natural childbirth" movement
clearly constituted a backlash against the medicalization of childbirth.
Yet in an increasingly urbanized country in the process of being dominated by a military-industrial complex, it also reflected a nostalgia for a
mythic yesteryear—a simpler, pastoral era when the demarcation
between domestic and public spheres was clear and women confined
themselves and their activities to the private realm. Dick-Read "glorified
motherhood as woman's true fulfillment in panegyrics" (Wertz and Wertz
1989, 183) that echoed the Victorian "cult of domesticity." He "associated motherhood with essential femininity, with purity, piety, and sub-
missiveness" (184). His goal was to reduce a woman's dependence on
anesthesia, thus enabling her to experience the "crowning moment of her
life . . . the divine moment" (185) when her child's cries heralded birth.
He focused on the primacy of "individual experience" (190), an emphasis that resonated in a country enamored of individualism. His exaltation
of motherhood coincided with media affirmations of the theme that a
"woman's place is in the home." Bette Davis and Joan Crawford invari-
ably traded their business suits for aprons, the approval of the board of
directors for true fulfillment as wives and mothers. After doing her patriotic duty, Rosie the Riveter, like her Revolutionary War counterpart, was
supposed to hand her drill over to a returning G.I. and retire to the nursery. And indeed, fertility rates increased in the 1950s.

The reaffirmation of traditional values and institutions in the aftermath of a brutal global conflict was epitomized in the romanticized
world of "Ozzie and Harriet." The dissonance between their cheery sub-
urban nest and the sterility of the hospital was jarring. Following publication in 1957 of a letter from a nurse criticizing "cruelty in maternity
wards" (Wertz and Wertz 1989, 170), the *Ladies Home Journal* was inun-
dated with letters complaining of dehumanizing treatment. A common
theme: "when the mother was ready to deliver, the staff was not ready to
attend" (Wertz and Wertz 1989, 170).

The chorus of criticism became ever louder once a new generation of
feminists emerged in the 1970s. As with the 1960s civil rights movement
from which it evolved, late twentieth-century feminism worked to
empower its constituency collectively and individually in defiance of culturally mandated roles and behaviors. "Our bodies, ourselves" became
the clarion call of the movement. Control of her own body constituted
the most essential expression of female empowerment: a woman should

have the right to consent to sex, to have an abortion, and to determine the circumstances of childbirth.

Notwithstanding traditional gender stereotypes articulated by earlier proponents of "natural childbirth," many feminists enthusiastically supported the cause, asserting that women should "reclaim childbirth" (Kahn 1995, 312). The hospital was characterized as a bastion of patriarchy presided over by physicians bent on "'control' rather than 'care'" (Oakley 1992, 13). "Captured by the routine and by the expertise surrounding them" in this inhumane environment, women had ceased to be the "main actors" in the drama of birth; instead, physicians "acted upon women's bodies" (Leavitt 1996, 252). Some activists advocated returning childbirth to the home, a space that in the nineteenth century had circumscribed and differentiated the world of women from that of men. This alternative was not always feasible or desirable for working-class and minority women, many of whom apparently welcomed a more "passive"(Wertz and Wertz 1989, 253) role in childbirth and continued to see the hospital as a respite from the stresses and responsibilities of their lives. As had been the case since the eighteenth century, women who were privileged, both in terms of education and "standard of living" (Michaelson 1988, 7) were forging a new paradigm of childbirth that largely reflected the goals and economic advantages of their class.

The "natural childbirth" movement made strange bedfellows of feminists and various pro-family groups who were otherwise unsympathetic, even hostile to each other. Their combined efforts succeeded in forcing modifications of the technocratic birth model, in part because competition within an overbuilt hospital system made administrators more customer-friendly; in part because physicians were persuaded of the advantage to the unborn child of techniques that might manage the mother's pain and thus reduce the use of anesthetics. A more inviting decor, birthing rooms, and, perhaps most importantly, the opportunity for significant others, relatives, and friends to support women throughout labor and delivery restored a more personal dimension to the hospital regimen. Yet, to the dismay of some, the "thralldom of birth to medicine" (Wertz and Wertz 1989, 283, italics mine) persisted. As implemented in a hospital environment, "natural" childbirth, in fact, was a hybrid of Lamaze, "episiotomy, outlet forceps, Demerol, and even epidural anesthesia" (Wertz and Wertz 1989, 195). Not only did the "natural childbirth" movement fail to displace the technocratic model, the "medicalization" of childbirth has become even more pervasive in recent years. Central to this phenomenon is the "discovery of the fetus" (Shorter 1982, 164) during the twentieth century, which occasioned a fundamental shift in the equilibrium between mother and infant.

The primacy of the male midwife after 1750 was a consequence of the prospect he offered of a safe delivery for mother *and* child. Even so, the focus of obstetrical interventions and innovations in the nineteenth and early twentieth centuries was on alleviating the mother's labor pain and eliminating threats to her health or survival. In the 1920s and 1930s the well-being of the fetus began to figure more prominently in the rationale for a variety of obstetrical procedures (Shorter 1982). DeLee's proposal in 1921 for the prophylactic use of forceps reflected this. Heretofore the rationale for an episiotomy was to prevent debilitating tearing of the perineum during labor. DeLee's technique required an episiotomy so forceps could extract the child from the vagina during the second stage in labor, ostensibly saving the child and mother from untold harm. By 1937 the high rate of episiotomies elicited this rationale from an obstetrical surgeon: "'The fetus is to be protected from the effects of a prolonged second stage, particularly from certain injuries which may result when the head acts as a dilator' [*sic*] of the mother's soft parts" (Shorter 1982, 172). The 1950 edition of *Williams Obstetrics* stated that the procedure "spares the baby's head the necessity of serving as a battering ram" (Shorter 1982, 172). During this same period, the well-being of the child was also referenced as part of the reasoning behind minimizing maternal weight gain and inducing or accelerating labor. Many doctors came to believe that "shortening a lengthy labor can prevent fetal brain damage" (Wertz and Wertz 1989, 261).

Once the traditional threats to the mother's health had been overcome, the focus on the fetus intensified. The history of cesarean surgery, a much more invasive procedure than episiotomy, encapsulates this development. Virtually synonymous with a "'death sentence'" (Shorter 1982, 161) prior to the development of anesthesia and antiseptic procedures, the technique was refined in the 1880s but sparingly used before the twentieth century in cases of obstructed births. Thereafter, cesareans, which require hospitalization, gradually replaced cutting through the pubic bone (symphysiotomy), high forceps delivery, or craniotomy in cases of obstruction because the procedure was less damaging to the mother than the traditional techniques. As late as 1956, *Williams Obstetrics* cautioned that the uterine scar from a cesarean might "rupture . . . in future pregnancies" (Shorter 1982, 175). That concern no longer prevailed by 1966, when the tome observed that "the focus of obstetric thinking" was on "infant survival and the prevention of trauma to the child during birth" (Shorter 1982, 175). By 1976 participants in an obstetrical association conference affirmed that "formerly focus was on the mother and delivery, and now it is centered on fetal outcomes." The increase in cesarean deliveries was attributable to the "desire to spare the fetus any trouble whatever" (Shorter 1982, 175). The percentage of cesarean deliveries went from 1 percent in the first decade of the twentieth century to 3.7 percent in the 1950s, 6.8 percent in the 1960s, 12.8 percent in the 1970s, and 24 percent by 1987 (Shorter 1982; Wertz and Wertz 1989). The growing utilization of the procedure hastened the exit of the general practitioner from the delivery room and also made feasible changes in recommendations about weight gain during pregnancy. A bigger baby, now thought to be a healthier, perhaps even a smarter baby, need not hazard the birth canal; it could instead be delivered by cesarean.

The obstetrical community's heightened interest in fetal development was reinforced by the parental quest for the perfect child as plummeting fertility rates from the 1960s onward enhanced the value of each infant. This same demographic trend prompted parents and their coterie to approach childbirth with often unrealistic expectations that were reinforced by television and movies. Since the experience might never be repeated, it, too, had to be perfect. The fact that two-career couples and single mothers often had limited time to devote to the long-term and unpredictable process of child rearing could predispose them to maximize the effort and emotion invested in the short-term process of pregnancy and childbirth, with its clearly defined timetable and procedures.

Notwithstanding a more ambivalent attitude toward science in the aftermath of Hiroshima, confidence in the perfectibility of the human condition through the manipulation of nature remained strong. Parents and physicians "collaborated" in a shared vision of the "perfect child" (Wertz and Wertz 1989, 268). A throwaway culture disdained the flawed, the imperfect. An increasingly litigious society had little tolerance for human frailty or mistakes. The threat of malpractice suits or other legal action served as subtext to the "American way of birth" in the late twentieth century. The quest for the perfect child generated a quantum increase in obstetrical technologies. Often intrusive procedures collided with efforts to enhance the quality of the birth experience for the mother. Genetic counseling, dietary strictures proscribing alcohol and smoking but favoring significant weight gain (notwithstanding potential postnatal weight-related problems for the mother), childbirth classes, ultrasound, amniocentesis, fetal monitors, antenatal surgery, and cesarean deliveries became commonplace. Entrepreneurs developed and touted increasingly complicated and costly medical technologies, and insurance companies paid the bills.

In pursuit of a perfect birth experience, Goldilocks has encountered Dr. Frankenstein. Neither are inclined to be risk-takers when the child is at stake. The "fetus, or an idea of the fetus . . . [has] assumed control of pregnancy and birth," to the point where mother and fetus can become "legal adversaries" (Wertz and Wertz 1989, 268, 269). Pregnant women can be incarcerated and even required to submit to highly invasive medical procedures if the best interests of a viable fetus is in question. At issue: "Does a woman have the right to satisfy her own needs for a certain type of birth experience, or does society's interest in the infant's safety outweigh her needs?" (Michaelson 1988, 120). Ironically, technology may resolve this conundrum. In the brave new world of the not too distant future, the petri dish and the incubator may eliminate "natural childbirth." Doting parents, camcorder in hand, will watch their genetically engineered, flawless offspring thrive in a medically contrived (and controlled) mechanical environment.

Issues of control, empowerment, and autonomy are preoccupations of the present more than of the past. The environmental and economic limitations of preindustrial society encouraged a fatalistic (Shorter 1982) outlook on the part of most people, including women in the throes of labor. Wertz and Wertz (1989) doubt that women ever had the degree of control over childbirth Leavitt posits in her history. And even Leavitt (1986) acknowledges that women's "authority" over childbirth was never "absolute." The unexpected could happen; there were "uncontrollable dangers" (210). The economic and technological promise of the twentieth century has profoundly altered popular expectations for prosperity and gratification, making possible the focus on personal fulfillment that fuels the current debate about the culture of childbirth.

In 1915 Margaret Llewelyn Davies published a collection of letters penned by British working-class women who had been asked to comment on their experience of maternity. At the time, Davies's volume provided a unique glimpse into the culture and concerns of "ordinary" women. At the cusp of the twenty-first century the voices of women from the mainstream are still surprisingly muted, whether drowned out or distorted by the sound and fury of zealots or ignored by cultural elites whose values and agendas often frame public debate on issues significant to all. The contemporary discourse on childbirth frequently juxtaposes natural and biomedical models as if they were irreconcilable. Such a dichotomy is fundamentally specious. In their research both Michaelson (1988) and Davis-Floyd (1992) found that many women favored a hybrid of the two approaches. The "birthing narratives" of such women can enrich our understanding of a fundamental human experience. If women from diverse ethnic, economic, and social backgrounds are given the opportunity to participate in defining a culture of childbirth for the new millennium, then we as a culture will have taken steps toward valuing, promoting, and protecting the interests of mother, child, and community. We will also have taken steps toward making better medical and political decisions. Such decisions, both personal and policy, possess the potential to shape the world of tomorrow in ways that can either enrich and ennoble or debase and dehumanize.

REFERENCES

Crawford, P. 1990. The construction and experience of maternity in seventeenth-century England. In *Women as mothers in pre-industrial England*, ed. V. Fildes, 3–38. London: Routledge.

Davies, M. L., ed. 1915. *Maternity: Letters from working women*. New York: W. W. Norton, 1978.

Davis-Floyd, R. E. 1988. Birth as an American rite of passage. In *Childbirth in America: Anthropological perspectives*, ed. K. Michaelson, 153–72. South Hadley, Mass.: Bergin & Garvey.

———. 1992. *Birth as an American rite of passage*. Berkeley: University of California Press.

———. 1996. The technocratic model of birth. In *The medicalization of obstetrics*, ed. P. Wilson, 247–76. New York: Garland. Reprinted from *Feminist theory and the study of folklore*, edited by S. T. Hollis et al., 297–326. Urbana: University of Illinois Press, 1993.

Forbes, T. 1996. The regulation of English midwives in the eighteenth and nineteenth centuries. In *The medicalization of obstetrics*, ed. P. Wilson, 32–42. New York: Garland. Reprinted from *Medical History* 15:352–62.

Gélis, J. [1984]. 1991. *History of childbirth: Fertility, pregnancy and birth in early modern Europe*, translated by R. Morris. Boston: Northeastern University Press.

Kahn, R. P. 1995. *Bearing meaning: The language of birth.* Urbana & Chicago: University of Illinois Press.

Kerber, L. K. 1980. *Women of the republic: Intellect and ideology in revolutionary America.* Chapel Hill: University of North Carolina Press.

King, C. 1996. The woman's experience of childbirth on the western frontier. In *Midwifery theory and practice,* ed. P. Wilson, 334–42. New York: Garland. Reprinted from *Journal of the West* 29 (1): 76–84.

Laslett, P. 1965. *The world we have lost.* New York: Scribners.

Leavitt, J. W. 1986. *Brought to bed: Childbearing in America 1750 to 1950.* New York: Oxford University Press.

———. 1996. "Science" enters the birthing room: Obstetrics in America since the eighteenth century. In *Midwifery theory and practice,* ed. P. Wilson, 231–54. New York: Garland. Reprinted from *Journal of American History* 70 (2): 281–304.

Lewis, J. 1986. *In the family way: Childbearing in the British aristocracy.* New Brunswick, N.J.: Rutgers University Press.

Marland, H., ed. 1993. *The art of midwifery: Early modern midwives in Europe.* London: Routledge.

Marland, H., and A. M. Rafferty, eds. 1997. *Midwives, society and childbirth.* London: Routledge.

Marx, L. 1964. *The machine in the garden: Technology and the pastoral ideal in America.* New York: Oxford University Press.

Michaelson, K. 1988. Childbirth in America: A brief history and contemporary issues. In *Childbirth in America: Anthropological perspectives,* ed. K. Michaelson, 1–32. South Hadley, Mass.: Bergin & Garvey.

Mitford, J. 1992. *The American way of birth.* New York: Dutton.

Oakley, A. 1984. *The captured womb: A history of the medical care of pregnant women.* United Kingdom: Basil Blackwell.

———. 1992. *Social support and motherhood: The natural history of a research project.* United Kingdom: Basil Blackwell.

Pollock, L. 1990. Embarking on rough passage: The experience of pregnancy in early-modern society. In *Women as mothers in pre-industrial England,* ed. V. Fildes, 39–67. London: Routledge.

Porter, R., and D. Porter. 1988. *In sickness and in health: The British experience 1650–1850.* Great Britain: Basil Blackwell.

Schnorrenberg, B. B. 1996. Is childbirth any place for a woman? The decline of midwifery in eighteenth-century England. In *Midwifery theory and practice,* ed. P. Wilson, 157–72. New York: Garland. Reprinted from *Studies in Eighteenth-Century Culture* 10:393–408.

Scholten, C. 1985. *Childbearing in American society: 1650–1850.* New York: New York University Press.

Shorter, E. 1982. *A history of women's bodies.* New York: Basic Books.

Stone, L. 1977. *The family, sex, and marriage in England, 1500–1800.* New York: Harper and Row.

Stowe, S. 1996. Obstetrics and the work of doctoring in the mid-nineteenth-century American south. In *Midwifery theory and practice,* ed. P. Wilson, 306–32. New York: Garland. Reprinted from *Bulletin of the History of Medicine* 64 (winter): 540–66.

Tew, M. 1990. *Safer childbirth? A critical history of maternity care.* London: Chapman & Hall.

Ulrich, L. T. 1996. "The living mother of a living child": Midwifery and mortality in post-revolutionary New England. In *Midwifery theory and practice,* ed. P. Wilson, 209–30. New York: Garland. Reprinted from *William and Mary Quarterly* 66 (1): 27–48.

Weintraub, S. 1987. *Victoria: An intimate biography.* New York: E. P. Dutton.

Wertz, D. 1996. What birth has done for doctors: A historical view. In *The medicalization of obstetrics,* ed. P. Wilson, 3–20. New York: Garland. Reprinted from *Women & Health* 8 (1): 7–24.

Wertz, R., and D. Wertz. 1989. *Lying-in: A history of childbirth in America.* Expanded ed. New Haven: Yale University Press.

Wilson, A. 1990. The ceremony of childbirth and its interpretation. In *Women as mothers in pre-industrial England,* ed. V. Fildes, 68–107. London: Routledge.

———. 1995. *The making of man-midwifery: Childbirth in England 1660–1770.* London: UCL Press.

———. 1996. The perils of early modern procreation: Childbirth with or without fear? In *Midwifery theory and practice,* ed. P. Wilson, 137–55. New York: Garland. Reprinted from *British Journal for Eighteenth-Century Studies* 16 (spring): 1–19.

2

BEARING WITNESS TO BIRTH
A Literary Perspective

Krista Ratcliffe

> One of the most startling omissions [in literature] is, of course, that of childbirth. . . . Given the number of novels in which childbirth is of central significance it is staggering to find that the event itself is virtually invisible. Women labor between the lines, children are born outside the pages, and rare even is the record of women's response[s]. . . .
> —Dale Spender, *The Writing or the Sex?*

> It is a subject on which nothing final can be known, so long as those who alone can really know it, women themselves, have given but little testimony, and that little, mostly suborned.
> —John Stuart Mill, "The Subjection of Women"

> [M]edical discourse and natural childbirth discourse are the two dominant or "official" discourses about childbirth in our culture. . . . There is also a third, marginalised, unofficial popular discourse whose echoes can be heard in women's accounts: the "old wives" tales—the oral tradition of women telling each other about childbirth.
> —Tess Cosslett, *Women Writing Childbirth*

Women's birthing narratives are routinely exiled from dominant discourses within the United States. Think about it for a moment. If a woman tells her birthing story during dinner, her companions may listen, sometimes intrigued, sometimes not, but they will almost certainly associate her with a lack of proper breeding (pun intended), except, perhaps, when they too are birthing women. Such pressure to exile women's birthing narratives results neither from a grand conspiracy nor from mere happenstance;

rather, it is a consequence of the ideology of birthing within the United States. Indeed, this discursive exiling occurs mostly unconsciously via three narrative moves: silencing, subornation, and marginalization. Dale Spender (1989) documents the silencing of women's birthing narratives in canonical literature; John Stuart Mill (1974) implies their subornations in popular culture[1]; and Tess Cosslett (1994) chronicles their marginalization into old wives' tales. As a result of these three moves, U.S. culture has a dearth of narratives that bear witness to birth.[2]

This dearth affects everyone—birthing women, nonbirthing women, men, and children—in terms of our socialization about birthing and gender. Our socialization promotes a myriad of problematic myths.[3] For example, TV and film present only two means of childbirth: birthing women are either safely ensconced within a hospital environment or dangerously trapped outside it. Such myths establish false expectations that affect actual experiences, as evidenced by the women interviewed for Helen Sterk's Birthing Project. As Sally D. (1996, 2) says, "I didn't feel like I was actively knowing what was going on in my body and allowing it to happen myself." So she put her faith in others. During labor and delivery she remembers thinking, "They are taking charge now. The baby will come because they are taking charge. They are doing what they are supposed to do and that means the baby will come when it's supposed to" (3). Such negative socialization angers Maria M. (1996, 15): "I just can't understand all these women who walk around and don't understand how this experience is being robbed from them all the time." Because such socialization shortchanges everyone, we need to resist the dominant ideology about birthing and promote an alternative one within which to reason and be socialized.

In the United States, the dominant ideology of birthing embraces two competing models: (1) the medical model, which valorizes technology and American Medical Association (AMA) protocols, and (2) the nostalgic natural childbirth model, which celebrates preindustrial nature. As Carla H. Hay's chapter has shown, within the medical model pregnancy functions within a disease metaphor, women's bodies function within a machine metaphor, and technology functions within a pregnancy-as-risk metaphor. As a result, a low-risk pregnancy is the best one can hope for, and technology is overused to prevent possible risks (including malpractice lawsuits). Hospital-affiliated natural childbirth classes may unwittingly serve this model, despite their stated agendas of putting women first, in that these classes often teach women strategies for making our hospital births and our doctor-patient relationships run more smoothly. A counter to the medical model, the nostalgic natural childbirth model eschews technology and advocates women giving birth on our own turf, trusting in nature and performing our own rituals before, during, and after birth. In a trickle-down fashion, the discourses of these two diametrically opposed models are translated into popular discourses about birthing, resulting in the afore-mentioned myths wherein women are portrayed either as totally dependent on doctors or totally in control of our bodies. For many women neither option is plausible or possible. So, ironically, despite their good intentions, both models perpetuate age-old tendencies to discount women's desires, denigrate our bodily experiences, and deny our right to tell our own stories.

Yet a third option does exist. Barbara Katz Rothman's *In Labor: Women and the Power in the Birthplace* (1982) offers a modern midwifery model in which the female body is perceived as the norm.[4] Within this model, *natural childbirth* means that informed mothers-to-be express their needs and that midwives (and, if necessary, doctors) read each woman's body to assess its needs and then proceed nonintrusively, using technology only when and if the situation (not AMA protocol) dictates, making decisions based on what women want and on what is best for the birthing woman and child. This modern midwifery model celebrates the experiential domain—that is, women's voices telling stories of birthing that have occurred on their own terms and in ways that challenge false myths as well as their consequences.

As Cosslett (1994, 4) reminds us, experientially based women's birthing narratives do indeed survive in the form of old wives' tales, "the oral tradition of women telling each other about childbirth." Analyzing these tales is com-plicated, however, for in the United States and elsewhere, old wives' tales do not stand *outside* dominant phallogocentric ideologies as representative of some essential womanhood; no discourse escapes history or ideology. Yet because "[r]esistance to ideology is inherent in every ideological stance" (Travis 1998, 5), these tales do sometimes stand *against* cultural tendencies to silence, suborn, and/or marginalize women's birthing narratives. In fact, lit-erary and lived "old wives' tales" are interesting case studies precisely because they are discursive sites of visibly contested agency wherein agency is accorded both to dominant discourses that socialize us and to the alternative discourses that challenge this socialization.

In this chapter, I explore these competing agencies by juxtaposing literary and lived old wives' tales. My purpose is to identify the narratives strategies un/consciously employed within U.S. culture to (1) exile women's birthing narratives and (2) return these narratives from exile.

JUXTAPOSING LITERARY AND LIVED BIRTHING NARRATIVES

As a methodology, juxtaposing literary and lived birthing narratives is fraught with assumptions. One concerns definition. As employed here, the term *narrative* signifies how we make sense of our world via storytelling.[5] The term *narrative strategies* refers to un/conscious rhetorical tactics of storytelling, for example, "teller, technique, story, situation, audience, and purpose" (Phelan 1996, 4). Women's *literary narratives* include fiction (novels, short stories, poems, and drama) and nonfiction (letters, journals, and essays); women's *lived narratives* refer to women's accounts of their actual experiences, specifically the Birthing Project interviews archived at Marquette University. A second assumption concerns premises. My main one is that women's bodies are valid sites of knowing. Although this idea seems common-sensical, cultural socialization in the United States actually screens out such body knowing, throwing suspicion on it despite several studies proving its existence and import (Jaggar and Bordo 1989; Marrone 1990; Smith 1996; Sorri 1989). A corollary premise is that women's body knowing may be articulated in literary and lived narratives. This idea concurs with contemporary research in psychoanalysis and cultural studies, which posits discourse (i.e., language in action) as a map, albeit an incomplete one, for analyzing the material body and its knowledge (Butler 1993). A third assumption concerns commonalities and distinctions between literary and lived narratives. Both function as discursive maps of personal and cultural views on birthing. Literary narratives offer ideologically situated representations of women's birthing experiences, distanced from women's experiences not only by language but by the genre of fiction and by the corporate editorial control exerted on fiction. Lived narratives offer ideologically situated representations of women's birthing experiences, removed from women's experiences not only by language and the subjects' skill with language but by the passage of time and the function of memory as well as by the intercessions of the ethnographer, the transcriber, and the editor.[6]

The challenge when analyzing literary and lived birthing narratives is twofold: (1) to locate discursive threads that reflect women's own narratives and not simply the dominant cultural logic, and (2) to discover gaps within the dominant cultural logic that women may fill with our own narratives so as to construct an alternative cultural logic.[7] This challenge is elucidated in Robbie Pfeufer Kahn's remarkable book, *Bearing Meaning: The Language of Birth* (1995, 36): "Finding words to describe the power of nurturance—the language of birth—is crucial to building models of partnership and mutual recognition. The challenge is to create narratives that do not reproduce the splits of Western descriptions of reality and do not replace one single-focused view with another." In sum, we should not simply replace the medical model with the nostalgic natural childbirth model; we should construct a model that enables women to tell our own stories.

Yet narrative poses certain challenges for women. It forces them to negotiate the questions: "What stories can be told? How can plots be resolved? What is felt to be narratable by both literary and social conventions?" (DuPlessis 1985, 3). It also forces them to negotiate a more radical question: How may such conventions be revised? To perform revisions, women must invent "transgressive . . . narrative strategies" (5), which interrupt "conventional structures of fiction and consciousness about women" (x). Some critics, like Cosslett (1994, 3), argue that revising narratives and narrative strategies evokes a "post-modern dilemma," in that feminist critics are torn between contradictory purposes: the need "to affirm women's [real] voices" and the need "to show how these voices . . . have been culturally constructed." This dilemma is a false one, however. Narrative revision is possible precisely because of how language functions: it "'bears us as we are born into it . . . '" (Marlatt, cited in Chester 1989b, 4). That is, both discourse and people possess agency: because we are born into cultural discourses with already established terms, definitions, and claims, discourse has the power to socialize our attitudes and actions; yet because we have the capacity to articulate and critique our socializations, we may choose to accept and/or to revise these discourses and their socializing effects. Granted, these two agencies are often difficult to distinguish. For even as we are born into language, language becomes embodied within us, with our bodies becoming inextricably encoded within a cultural network of signifying systems. Yet because a birthing woman does possess agency (however partial), she has, in terms of narrative, "the power to take over the story; in terms of childbirth, the power to control the experience; or, in both cases, the power to protest, or celebrate, lack of control" (Chester 1989b, 3).

Still, revising narratives and narrative strategies is not a simple process: we do not simply step outside history or cultural logics; we revise from within. Revising narratives and narrative strategies is also not a cure-all solution, for by changing language we do not automatically change people and culture. Yet because cultural beliefs are discursively constructed, we can deconstruct dominant narratives and revise them to effect possibilities for personal and social change. To effect such possibilities for change in terms of our birthing socialization, we must first ask: What narrative strategies are un/consciously employed to send women's birthing narratives into exile?

EXILE: SILENCING, SUBORNING, AND MARGINALIZING WOMEN'S BIRTHING NARRATIVES

Within the United States, people are socialized to believe that birthing and discussions about birthing should be private, contained within a home or a hospital. Consequently, knowledge about birthing does not emerge as part of our cultural "common sense." So when birthing narratives do invade public spheres, a common reaction is disgust. For example, after reading Enid Bagnold's *The Squire* (a 1938 novel whose plot centers around birthing from a mother's point of view), H.G. Wells claimed that he felt as if he had "'been attacked by a multitude of many-breasted women . . . and thrown into a washing basket full of used nursery napkins . . .'" (cited in Cosslett 1994, 1). Although Wells's example may be an extreme reaction, U.S. college women also manifest this disgust, as noted by the persona in Alicia Ostriker's (1989c, 25) "Propaganda Poem: Maybe for Some Young Mamas":

> (after reading the girls my old pregnancy poem
> that I thought ripe and beautiful
> after they made themselves clear it was ugly
> after telling the girls I would as soon
> go to my grave a virgin, god
> forbid, as go to my grave without
> ever bearing and rearing a child
> I laughed
> and if looks could kill I would
> have been one dead duck in that
> so-called 'feminist' classroom)

This disgust both reflects and reinforces a cultural tendency in the United States to exile women's birthing narratives to a private sphere via silencing, subornation, and marginalization. These not-so-innocent practices occur via five narrative strategies. To illustrate these five strategies, I draw on a variety of genres, for example, philosophical dialogues, drama, poetry, academic research, novels, self-help books, and ethnographic transcripts. I also draw on a variety of Western texts from different cultures and different historical moments. My point is not to deny the specificity of each genre, the historicity of each text, or the differences within and among these texts. Rather, my primary purpose is to demonstrate how these texts are threads woven into contemporary U.S. culture. My corollary purpose is to demonstrate that these five un/conscious strategies of exile are as old as recorded Western history and as recent as today.

STRATEGY #1: REMOVING BIRTH FROM THE PHYSICAL REALM

The most ingenious strategy of exile is erasing women from the birthing process by removing birth from the physical realm and rendering it metaphorical (DuBois 1988; Kahn 1995; Mossman 1993). Plato popularized this trend in the *Phaedrus* (trans. 1977) with his concept of Platonic love. According to Socrates, Platonic lovers should base their love not on physical, bodily, homoerotic passions but on metaphysical, nonbodily, rational exchanges: "words about justice and beauty and goodness spoken by teachers for the sake of instruction and really written in a soul . . . should be considered the speaker's own legitimate offspring, first the word within himself, if it be found there, and secondly its descendants or brothers which may have sprung up in worthy manner in the souls of others" (573–75). In other words, the Platonic lover plants his seed (his ideas) in a fertile womb (another's mind) in order to beget offspring (a soul's remembrance of ideal truths)—all of which occurs sans blood and women's bodies. In this way, Plato divorces birth from the physical and "elevates" it to the metaphysical via metaphor, thus acknowledging the primordial power of birthing while abrogating women's connection with it.

Removing birth from the physical realm by rendering it metaphorical reinforces patriarchal commonplaces of birthing. One commonplace posits birth as a metaphor for the physical violence that leads to social change. This metaphoric link is exemplified in Aeschylus's *Oresteia* (trans. 1975, 141), specifically the *Agamemnon*, when the chorus cries, "Justice comes to birth—." This line foretells both Clytemnestra's impending murder of her husband Agamemnon and their son Orestes' eventual murder of her. Interestingly, the chorus's line may be read in diametrically opposed ways: Clytemnestra's killing of Agamemnon (in return for his earlier ritual sacrifice of their daughter Iphigenia) may be read as justice within a revenge-based matriarchy; conversely, or more popularly, Clytemnestra's action may be read as a necessary step toward establishing a law-based patriarchy. In either case, birth is associated with violent change in a social order.

A second patriarchal commonplace makes birthing a metaphor for pain and terror. This metaphoric link is again exemplified in Aeschylus's *Oresteia* (trans. 1975, 151), in the scene where Cassandra foresees the deaths of Agamemnon and herself: "Aieeeee!—/ the pain, the terror! The birth-pang of the seer / who tells the truth—it whirls me, oh, / the storm comes again, the crashing chords!" Though compellingly dramatic, this birthing metaphor invokes only negative elements of birthing and inverts the process to signify death, not life.

A third patriarchal commonplace metaphorically links birth to artistic creation. After studying birthing metaphors in literary works by women and men, Susan Stanford Friedman (1987, 51–52) concluded that birthing metaphors have traditionally worked against women: they evoke "the sexual division of labor upon which Western patriarchy is founded. The vehicle of the metaphor (procreation) acts in opposition to the tenor it serves (creation) because it inevitably reminds the reader of the historical realities that contradict the comparison being made." If birthing metaphors always turn our gazes back to women's wombs, then men writers (who have no wombs upon which to gaze) have needed to worry only about creating books. Women writers, however, have been trapped within an unthinkable dichotomy—whether to create babies or books:

> Ellen Glasgow, for example, recalled the advice of a literary man: "The best advice I can give you is to stop writing and go back to the South and have some babies. The greatest woman is not the woman who has written the finest book, but the woman who has had the finest babies." Male paternity of texts has not precluded their paternity of children. Yet for both material and ideological reasons, maternity and creativity have appeared to be mutually exclusive to women writers. (Friedman 1987, 52)

These uses of literary birthing metaphors sustain the split between metaphysical and physical as well as between the artistic potential of men and women.[8] Although women have indeed written *and* had babies, they have done so only because they have challenged dominant cultural logics.

STRATEGY #2: ELIMINATING WOMEN FROM
THE PHYSICAL PROCESS OF BIRTH

Another strategy for exiling birthing narratives is eliminating women from the birthing process, specifically maintaining its physical dimension but allotting it to men. Such a move is evidenced in the myth of Athena, the Greek and Roman goddess of war and wisdom. In the following description of Athena's birth, note how her mother is never mentioned: "[Athena] sprang from the brain of Jove [Zeus], agleam with panoply of war, brandishing a spear and with her battle-cry awakening the echoes of heaven and earth" (Gayley 1939, 23). Athena's missing mother is Metis, the goddess of wisdom, who was swallowed by Zeus after he impregnated her with Athena. In this rapaciously cannibalistic move, Zeus co-opts Metis' domains not just of birthing but of wisdom. As a result, Athena emerges from Zeus's forehead as a male-identified daughter, a goddess representing both patriarchal reasoning (wisdom) and the breakdown of such reasoning (war). Sadly, Athena repeats her father's strategy of eliminating women: "With Athena's help Apollo denies the mother's procreative role: 'The mother is not the true parent of the child / which is called hers. She is a nurse who tends the growth / of young seed planted by its true parent, the male'" (Hirsch 1989, 30). Sadly, U.S. culture repeats Zeus and Athena's strategy of eliminating women every time we assign a child his father's name but not his mother's, every time we give the father the "last word" in disciplining a child, and every time we take a mother's care for granted while praising a father's participation.[9]

STRATEGY #3: OMITTING BIRTHING WOMEN'S POINTS OF VIEW

The most common strategy of exile is omitting birthing women's points of view and representing them as observed objects. A birthing woman does not speak for herself; a male-identified narrator or character speaks for her. This strategy is especially common in narratives where the births of important men are integral to the plotline. Consider, for example, the birth of Prince Nicholas Andréevich in Leo Tolstoy's *War and Peace* (trans. 1952). In the chapter where Princess Lise gives birth to Prince Nicholas, the narrator romantically objectifies Lise and then speaks for her:

> The little princess lay supported by pillows, with a white cap on her head (the pains had just left her). Strands of her black hair lay round her

inflamed and perspiring cheeks, her charming rosy mouth with its downy
lip was open and she was smiling joyfully. Prince Andrew [her husband]
entered and paused facing her at the foot of the sofa on which she was
lying. Her glittering eyes, filled with childlike fear and excitement, rested
on him without changing their expression. "I love you all and have done
no harm to anyone; why must I suffer so? Help me!" *her look seemed to say*
[italics added]. (182)

Whether or not Lise really thinks what "her look seemed to say" is never
questioned, for almost immediately the narrator ushers the doctor into
the birthing room and readers into an adjoining room to await with
Prince Andrew the news of Lise's confinement. With him, we hear her
shriek, the baby's shriek, then silence. Afterward, the doctor leaves without
a word, and Prince Andrew enters the birthing room and looks upon his
wife, who no longer has the opportunity to speak for herself, for she is
now "lying dead, in the same position he had seen her in five minutes
before and, despite the fixed eyes and the pallor of the cheeks, the same
expression was on her charming childlike face with its upper lip covered
with tiny black hairs" (183). In both scenes, the reader knows Lise's
birthing experience only from what the male-identified narrator and other
characters can observe; thus, Lise exists for readers as an observed object,
not a knowing subject.

Ironically, representations of women as observed objects permeate
women's "self-help" books, too. Cosslett (1994, 9) urges us not to forget
how Grantly Dick Read ("the 'father' of the modern natural childbirth
movement") constructed the "primitive" woman's birthing process. This
romanticized version portrays lower-class, usually nonwhite female bodies
pausing from their hoeing, squatting in the field for a few relatively painless moments, then continuing their work with their babies on their backs.
Although this image has been challenged by several anthropologists, it still
lives in the popular imagination. Note how a young unmarried mother in
Toi Derricotte's *Natural Birth* (1989, 109) fantasizes about keeping her
child: "I would squat down and deliver just like the / peasants in the field,
shift my baby to my back, and / continue. . . ." Although this pervasive
myth has deleterious effects on the material lives of all women, it engenders definite differences about how close to nature or how removed from
it particular women are. Not surprisingly, these different representations
are often based on a woman's race and class and her country's industrialized status. Western, industrialized, white women are perceived by the

dominant culture (and often by themselves) as separated from nature and not very intuitive about birthing; non-Western, nonindustrialized, non-white women are perceived by the dominant culture as closer to nature and more intuitive. What's missing in these perceptions is (1) the differences among white women and among women of color; (2) the existence of women of color in industrialized nations and the existence of white women in nonindustrialized ones; and (3) the fact that women of color in the United States have historically had to be more knowledgeable about birthing than their white counterparts because they have been denied the information, technology, and access that, in some cases, might have made their birthing safer and their babies' life expectancies longer.

STRATEGY #4: OFFERING PARTIAL ACCOUNTS OF BIRTHING WOMEN'S POINTS OF VIEW

Even when a birthing woman's point of view is included, it is often only a partial account. For example, in George Moore's best-selling nineteenth-century English novel *Esther Waters* (1983), which broke Victorian taboos by tracing the life of a servant who fights for the life of her illegitimate son, the birthing scene provides us only a partial view of Esther's impressions.[10] Granted, in the moments preceding the birth, the narrator does take us inside Esther's head:

> The last pain had so thoroughly exhausted her that she had fallen into a doze. But she could hear the chatter of the nurses so clearly that she did not believe herself asleep. And in this film of sleep reality was distorted, and the unsuccessful operation which the nurses were discussing Esther understood to be a conspiracy against her life. She awoke, listened, and gradually sense of the truth returned to her. She was in the hospital, and the nurses were talking of someone who had died last week. . . .
>
> Suddenly, the discussion was interrupted by a scream from Esther; it seemed to her that she was being torn asunder, that life was going from her. (124–25)

Yet moments later, when the baby begins moving down the birth canal, the narrator shifts his point of view so that Esther, like Lise, becomes object, not subject. That is, the narrator observes Esther first from the nurse's point of view, then from the doctor's, with only a brief insight from Esther herself before she succumbs to the anesthesia:

The nurse ran to her side, a look of triumph came upon her face, and she said "Now, we shall see who's right," and forthwith went for the doctor. He came running up the stairs; silence and scientific collectedness gathered round Esther, and after a brief examination he said, in a low whisper: "I'm afraid this will not be as easy a case as one might have imagined. I shall administer chloroform."

He placed a small wire case over her mouth and nose. The sickly odor which she breathed from the cotton wool filled her brain with nausea; it seemed to choke her; life faded a little, and at every inhalation she expected to lose sight of the circle of faces. (Moore 1983, 124–25)

Esther's partial point of view is most obvious in the actual moment of birth. Once she succumbs to the chloroform, the author breaks the narrative with a white space. Until this point in the novel, white spaces occur only as chapter breaks; in this birthing scene, however, the white space interrupts the narrative midchapter. One might argue that this textual break is literarily appropriate: because Esther is unconscious via chloroform, she (and thus we as readers) cannot know what is happening to her. Yet there are other instances in the text where the narrator shifts from Esther's point of view to other characters' points of view (e.g., the nurse's and doctor's in the above excerpt). Why then does the narrator relegate the actual birth to a white space? More than just a nod to Victorian sensibility, this white space may be read as Western culture's transhistorical loathing of the fluids, functions, and physicality of the female body. Moreover, this white space reflects another cultural assumption about birth: it is something that has to be done *to* a woman *by* those with expert knowledge.

Not only is the birth partially erased; so too are Esther's postpartum experiences. Moments (hours?) after the actual birth, the narrator makes readers once again privy to Esther's thoughts, yet we are given little information about her physical or emotional condition. Instead, the narrative focus shifts from Esther to her baby. When Esther emerges from the anesthesia, she realizes, along with the reader, that the birth has already occurred: "And then the darkness began to lighten; night passed into dawn; she could hear voices, and when her eyes opened the doctors and nurses were still standing round her, but there was no longer any expression of eager interest on their faces. She wondered at this change, and then out of the silence there came a tiny cry" (Moore 1983, 125). When she is given her baby for the first time, her thoughts are only for her child:

"Its eyes were open; it looked at her, and her flesh filled with a sense of happiness so deep and so intense that she was like one enchanted. And when she took the child in her arms she thought she might die of happiness" (125–26). Subsequently, although the narrator tells us that Esther must remain in the hospital for a three-week recovery, the only detail we are given is that "[a]ll her joints were loosened" (126).

Although partial knowledge is better than erasure, it still fosters misguided views about women's bodies and birthing. In Esther's case, it also leaves us with questions: What joints are loose? How loose are they? Will they tighten again? And what does *loose* mean? By criticizing such partial views of birthing, I am not arguing for a grand narrative that neatly explains all things related to birth; I am, however, arguing for an expanded repertoire of views that includes birthing women's.

STRATEGY #5: DISCOUNTING WOMEN'S BIRTHING NARRATIVES AS OLD WIVES' TALES

In medical discourses, old wives' tales are discounted as nonscientific. Associated with midwives and birthing women, such tales are perceived as predicated upon an unreliable sampling and a trial-and-error methodology. The status of these tales in medical discourses directly affects their status in popular discourses, and the status of old wives' tales in popular discourses directly affects the material status of women. In *Of Woman Born*, Adrienne Rich (1986) links the devaluation of women's birthing experiences in the West to male physicians' appropriation of midwifery. Rich cites as evidence the situation of Anne Hutchinson, an American Puritan midwife who was seen as "threatening and subversive" (135) not only because she conducted theology classes for women, thus interfering with the tradition of men's revealing the gospel to women, but also because she was perceived as having midwifery powers over life and death and sexuality, for example, providing either aphrodisiacs or charms to induce impotence, depending upon her patients' desires.

Despite the recent resurgence of midwifery in the United States, the medical establishment is still devaluing midwives' powers while appropriating their function. As nurse-midwife Carol Niemczura explains, in recent years midwives have challenged most doctors' wishes and assisted women wanting vbac's (vaginal births after cesarean); currently doctors are arguing that vbac's may be safe but only if supervised by a doctor (personal conversation, 21 March 1998; also see Richards 1987). Midwife devaluation also occurs more subtly. The best-selling *What to Expect When You're Expecting* (Eisenberg, Murkoff, and Hathaway 1991), a manual that ob/gyns frequently give to their pregnant patients, offers midwifery as an option for labor and delivery, yet the author's language belies a certain hesitancy:

> If you are looking for a practitioner whose emphasis is on you the person and not you the patient, who will take extra time to talk with you about your feelings and problems, who will be oriented toward the "natural" in childbirth, then a certified nurse-midwife (CNM) may be right for you (though, of course, many physicians meet these requirements too). Although a nurse-midwife is a medical professional, thoroughly trained to care for women with low-risk pregnancies and to attend uncomplicated births (having received special education, training, and certification in midwifery), she is more likely to treat your pregnancy as a human, rather than a medical, condition. If you choose a midwife, be sure she's certified; a lay midwife cannot provide you and your baby with optimal care. (10)

While I am the last to ridicule how advancements in medical knowledge and technology have made childbearing safer for some women, I am concerned about the dominant metaphors and dichotomies in this passage—and, by extension, in medical, natural childbirth, and popular discourses. Note how "risk" defines the entire process, with a "low-risk" pregnancy being the best one can hope for. Such metaphors might work against women, their babies, their families, and even their doctors, defining the categories within which to reason and, thus, limiting what is possible and impossible to imagine. I am also concerned about the dominant dichotomies. Midwives can deal with "persons," not "patients"; they will invoke "natural," not "scientific" processes; they are "trained" but only for "low-risk" pregnancies, not "high-risk" ones; they know about "human," not "medical" conditions; finally, they must be "certified," not "lay." Within such discourses, doctors are those-who-know, midwives are those-who-sometimes-know, and birthing women are those-who-do-not-know.

To challenge such discursive socialization, we must now ask: How may women's birthing narratives be returned from exile? To explore this question, I turn to narrative strategies that women have employed to give voice to silenced birthing narratives, to revise suborned accounts, and to invite marginalized accounts into the center as well as to reimagine what constitutes the center.

A Return from Exile: Articulating Narrative Strategies in Women's Literary and Lived Birthing Stories

Women who tell birthing stories may both reinforce and challenge patriarchy's exiling of women's birthing narratives. Women writers reinforce this exile when they shy "away from the subject of pregnancy and birth, possibly afraid that men might judge it 'limited,' too focused on the processes of the body" (Chester 1989b, 2). The irony, of course, is that birthing and mothering provide "direct access to the greatest themes in literature—birth, death, loss, love" (Chester 1989b, 4), as in Toni Morrison's *Beloved* (1988). Yet women writers have challenged this exile when they have written women-centered birthing narratives. To explain *how* these challenges have been enacted in literary and lived birthing narratives, I identify six narrative strategies. Others no doubt exist. My purpose is not to delineate a totality of strategies but to enter a conversation that needs to be continued.

Strategy #1: Re/Defining Terms

The most obvious term to re/define is *birth*. For the narrator in Margaret Atwood's short story "Giving Birth" (1989), the crucial redefinition questions are: how does *birth* function grammatically?—that is, "who gives it? And to whom is it given?" (80); and how does *birth* function logically?— that is, "How can you be both the sender and the receiver at once?" (80). To these two questions I would add a third: How does *birth* function philosophically—that is, how can a culture so enamored of a self that is autonomous and unified allot space for discussions of two selves existing in one body or of one body dividing into two selves? (Cosslett, 1994, 8). These contradictions belie the insufficiency of our language and dominant cultural logics to capture women's experiences. Indeed, these contradictions signal the need to re/name women's experiences, especially those related to birth.

It is worth noting that Atwood's questions—and mine—emerge from a decidedly Western cultural logic, one that celebrates neat categorizations, clear-cut definitions, and binary oppositions. In *Lakota Woman*, Mary Crow Dog offers an alternative cultural logic within which to define *birth*. In a chapter entitled "Birth Giving," she explains that the "Sioux language has a number of words for pregnancy. One of them means 'growing strong.' Another means 'to be overburdened'" (Crow Dog and

Erdoes 1990, 157). By inverting the term *giving birth* into *birth giving* and promoting multiple and oppositional definitions of pregnancy, Crow Dog not only preserves her cultural history and logic but also challenges readers to critique the categories, definitions, and oppositions haunting Western logic.

Yet whether we look to Atwood or Crow Dog to redefine *birth,* Carol Mossman (1993) warns us that such redefining will not be easy:

> How to begin a study of birth? Merely to mention birth summons up branches of knowledge as diverse as medical science and bio-ethics, psychology, theology, anthropology, political science, and aesthetics, to name only a few. For birth cannot be contemplated in isolation: to speak of birth is to open up the problematics of origins. And culture has a stake in addressing origins. This much is evident from the universal existence of myths and cosmogonies which recount genesis. To the extent that such accounts also seek to situate human existence within the larger scheme of things, narratives of collective origins must intertwine with what it means for the individual to emerge into the world. (1)

Birth must be reimagined in ways that account for the intertwinings of personal subjectivities and cultural structures. Many literary and lived birthing narratives have done just that.

To expose the personal and cultural implications of birthing, women have redefined *birth* as making love. In Summer Brenner's poem "Blissed Raga" (1989a, 41), a woman tells the persona: "Honey that baby is what I call making love."[11] This claim not only aptly defines *birth* as "making" a baby who may personify love; it also exposes the shallowness of our common usage of "making love" to mean "having sex." Alicia Ostriker's "Propaganda Poem" (1989c) further unpacks the personal and cultural implications of the love that birth makes. Ostriker's poem links birth and love with fun: "I am telling you and you can take me for a fool there is no / good time like the good time a whole mama / has with a whole little baby" (27). It also links birth and love with the origin of deity: " . . . and that's / where the first images / of deity came from—sister you know it's true" (27). And it links birth and love with joy: "the joy that hurts nobody / the dazzling circuit of contact without dominance / that by the way might make you less vulnerable / to cancer and who knows what other diseases / of the body / because who can bear a thing that makes you happy / and rolls the world a little way / on forward / toward its destiny" (27).

To expose the personal and cultural implications of birth, women have also redefined *birth* as an intersubjective experience, exposing a cross-cultural desire of birthing bodies for other bodies. Sometimes those other bodies are friends or nurses or doctors in a hospital setting, as in Laura Chester's "The Stone Baby" (1989e): "With Martine's encouragement, and the nurse's optimism, Dr. Chou's kind face, things progressed" (127). Sometimes those other bodies work in a birthing center, as in Lee H.'s interview (1996, 16): "the essential thing a doula brings to a birth [is] having another caring person there to help carry the load.'" Yet sometimes those other bodies are complete strangers, as in Morrison's *Beloved* (1988), where the escaped black slave Sethe Suggs is assisted in her labor by the escaped white indentured servant Amy Denver: "On a riverbank in the cool of a summer evening two women struggled under a shower of silvery blue. They never expected to see each other again in this world and at the moment couldn't care less. But there on a summer night surrounded by bluefern they did something together appropriately and well" (85). What's most important, according to Molly S. (1996, 15) in her interview, is that "[y]ou have to have someone there who can really advocate for you."

This intersubjectivity also links personal and cultural implications of birthing to the flow of time. This intersubjectivity may mark the present, as it does in Laura Chester's *Primagravida* (1989c, 203): "I'm lying here *now* with part of my own body, part of us . . ." (emphasis mine). It may weave backward in time, making birthing women realize that their babies are both a connection to and the culmination of millions of years of women's birthing. Erica Jong describes this realization in "On the First Night" (1989, 124): the birthing mother remembers "pushing you out of myself / as my mother / pushed / me out of herself, / as her mother did, / & her mother's mother before her, / all of us born / of woman." This intersubjectivity also may weave into the future, for babies do not stay babies; they grow up, have their own children, and eventually die, as Sheryl Jaffe (1989b, 260) describes in "Something Larger": "They themselves began to age. They didn't know what to make of it. . . . Their children came to them and gathered round them. And finally they had to surrender. There was another presence in the room. Something larger."

Once a woman experiences this intersubjectivity, she returns to herself the same yet different. Elise N. (1996, 37) notes in her interview, "M's birth has been a very symbolic rebirth for me in a lot of ways. And I find myself looking at the world differently"; moreover, Elise "was surprised and maybe a little disappointed that it wasn't more of an obviously cosmic experience for [her husband]." This difference sometimes takes a spiritual turn. Toi Derricotte's persona in *Natural Birth* (1989, 115) claims, "we were through the pain, would never suffer in our / lives again. put pain down like a rag, unzipper skin, / step out of our dead bodies, and leave them on the / floor. glorious spirits were rising, blanched with / light, like thirsty women shining with their thirst." This difference also sometimes takes a demystifying turn, enabling women to see our bodies in a new light. In her interview, Sarah Jane C. (1996, 22) admits that birthing, "was a huge breakthrough for me because I had a lot of these body image issues from the time I was a kid. It was very healing for me."

Such reimagined concepts of birth expose the lifelong, holistic implications of birthing. Helen Sterk reinforced this idea in the Birthing Project by adopting a four-part interview pattern that defines *birth* as (1) experiences of pregnancy, (2) experiences of labor and delivery, (3) experiences after the baby is born, and (4) any advice the interviewees wish to offer. The latter is especially important in interrupting the nine-month linear model of birthing and demonstrating birthing's intersections with all aspects of women's lives—from mothering to being a daughter, from jobs to friendships, from religious practices to sex, from life to death. Expanding this idea, Rich (1986) redefines *childbirth* as an always already ongoing process:

> [It] is (or may be) one aspect of the entire process of a woman's life, beginning with her own expulsion from her mother's body, her own sensual suckling or being held by a woman, through her earliest sensations of clitoral eroticism and of the vulva as a source of pleasure, her growing sense of her own body and its strengths, her masturbation, her menses, her physical relationship to nature and to other human beings, her first and subsequent orgasmic experiences with another's body, her conception, pregnancy, to the moment of first holding her child. But that moment is still only a point in the process if we conceive it not according to patriarchal ideas of childbirth as a kind of production, but as part of female experience.
>
> Beyond birth comes nursing and physical relationship with an infant, and these are enmeshed with sexuality, with the ebb and flow of ovulation and menses, of sexual desire. (182–83)

Rather than reducing childbirth to a disease (a practice of many insurance companies) or compartmentalizing it into a nine-month section of a woman's life (a practice of many employers), Rich's definition collapses time and experience in ways that celebrate childbirth as both a particular moment and a wave of life. In her interview, Lee H. (1996) confirms Rich's claim about birthing's wave function:

> I remember taking a shower with [my daughter] about 3 days after she was born and loving my body. You know how women hate their bodies? We have too much bosom or too little bosom or we're too hippy or we're short-waisted? . . . I remember thinking, "My body is wonderful. It has done this amazing thing," and I never felt the same about myself physically or emotionally again. It was a transformational event in my life. (15)

We should all heed her insight.

STRATEGY #2: RE/IMAGINING THE GROUNDS OF ANALYSIS AND KNOWLEDGE

When redefining *birth*, we must also redefine the grounds from which the term arises. Within the medical model, medical institutions and medically trained experts are the primary sites of knowledge. As a result, birthing women have been, and often still are, denied control over their birthing processes. For example, the narrator in Derricotte's *Natural Birth* (1989) describes how the nurse continually offers to give her a shot and how the doctor "keeps coming in, / making me hurt, sticking his whole hand up my asshole" in what feels like a rape (112). Laurie Colwin's *Another marvelous thing* (1989) continues this rape metaphor when the narrator describes a "delivery": "Billy's arms were taped, her legs were numb, and a clear plastic mask was placed over her nose and mouth. She was so frightened she wanted to cry out, but it was impossible. Instead she breathed as Katherine Walden had taught her to. Every time a wave of panic rose, she breathed it down" (116–17). Then, to add insult to injury, Billy is separated from her under-five-pound baby: "'Please let me have him,' Billy said. 'He'll be fine,' Eva said. They then took him away" (117). Note how in Derricotte's text, the nurse and the doctor are in the subject position of the sentences as agents of action while the birthing woman receives the action; also note how in Colwin's text, the birthing woman is in the subject position, but given the passive voice construction, she remains the recipient of another's action.

To combat their relegation to passive roles, birthing women have been searching for alternative cultural logics wherein their own bodies become the grounds of knowledge.[12] If we are to conceptualize birthing women's bodies as grounds of knowledge, Mossman (1993) argues that we must "historicize and denaturalize an institution so often presented as a phenomenon of Nature opposite to Culture" (9). To historicize and denaturalize birth, Mossman exposes the links between birth and other culturally constructed concepts: for example, the Maternal, politics, gender, the Judeo-Christian tradition, and the Self. The Self provides a particularly fruitful means for reimagining women's bodies as grounds of knowledge, because Western narratives lack a category for Self in relation to women's two-in-one birthing bodies. According to Mossman, "the act of birth serves the narratological function of aggrandizing an extraordinary individual, casting a mystique about his very origins. The origins of the female self, however, can hardly be said to belong to any such convention" (4). Mossman's analysis exposes not only that women's births have rarely forwarded plots in canonical literature or in political, intellectual, or economic histories but also that women's bodies must be reconceptualized in relation to the Self.

Not surprisingly, women writers have done just that, positing women's bodies as sites of un/conscious knowing. Such body knowing may occur at any time during birthing. It may emerge immediately after conception, as in Carol Bergé's *Acts of Love* (1989, 182): "Ellen was pregnant. She knew it from the third day after she conceived. . . . She was startled; she *knew.*" It may continue during pregnancy, as in Karina K.'s ethnographic account (1996, 4) of her abusive relationship: "We had gotten into a fight and he was chasing me around the house and I remember distinctly telling him, 'You are not going to hurt my baby.' I don't know where that came from. It just came out of my mouth. I knew that I shouldn't let anything happen to myself." It may repeat during transition, as Lee H. (1996, 22) reports in her ethnographic account of a conversation she had with herself during birthing wherein her use of "I" reveals a split between what her mind and body know: "I started thinking, 'Body, do you feel like pushing?' 'No, I guess I don't.' The next contraction hit and I suddenly went, 'Argh. Now I do.'" This body knowing may announce delivery, as in Margaret Atwood's "Giving Birth" (1989, 89): "Suddenly she sits bolt upright. She is wide awake and lucid. 'You have to ring that bell right now,' she says. 'This baby is being born.'" It may also herald the end of delivery, as in Morrison's *Beloved* (1988, 85): "When a foot rose from the river bed and kicked the bottom of the boat and Sethe's behind, she knew it was done and permitted herself a short faint." When women describe body-knowing Selves, they express wonder and astonishment. Yet what is really astonishing is that our socialization either divorces us from such knowing or makes us highly suspicious of it. Rarely do we simply accept Molly S's advice (1996, 12): "The main thing is your body knows exactly what to do. Let your body do the work. Relax, don't fight against your body."

Because many women feel that the medical model denigrates their birthing experiences, a body-knowing Self challenges the knowledge of the medical model. In her interview, Elise N. (1996) tells of having two children by c-section because doctors confused her vaginal ring with her cervix and assumed her cervix was not dilated enough for a vaginal birth. Because she did not have the language and hence the knowledge of these differences, she could not contradict the doctors' decisions. Elise then tells of having her third child vaginally because a nurse could feel the difference and, thus, detect her cervical dilation of ten centimeters. Elise's anger about her first two experiences still haunts her: "I understand that in obstetrics a failed outcome is the greatest tragedy. I understand that. And I understand that people in that situation are perhaps even more methodological than they would be in any other kind of medical situation. But I don't think that means that the . . . the . . . the consequence of that then is that women will have cesarean sections as a matter of form which is almost what's happening now" (34). Elise's anger is complicated by the medical practice available to her during her first two pregnancies: "it makes me angry that there is a system like at _____ where you don't get to see the same physician twice in a row. Where you can't have a human relationship. Because I am convinced that was one of the key differences between the first two [births] and the third one" (33). Other interviewees echo suspicion of the medical model's knowledge. Sage B. (1996, 11) asserts: "I really am a believer that medical intervention for the most part is not necessary and tends to throw your body off track." Lee H. (1996, 27) concurs: "Trust your inner wisdom. . . . Trust your instincts."

By challenging the knowledge of the medical model, a body-knowing Self also challenges its authority, raising questions of who can speak and who can be heard. The problem is not simply a doctor's silencing a woman or not hearing her when she does speak. It also includes the system that trains doctors and, sometimes, even the system that trains women to give birth in hospitals. It also includes women's internalizing this message and either not speaking or not rebelling when they speak and are not heard. For example, Lee H. (1996) recounts in her interview the ease with which she accepted medical personnel's urgings not to gain more than twenty pounds—"I would go hungry sometimes because I was a good, cooperative patient" (1); she also recounts the ease with which she accepted their urgings to take tranquilizers during labor—"I was very compliant so I took it" (2). In either case, she did not and could not imagine saying "No." Emmy B. (1996) describes in her interview a botched episiotomy that left a tiny hole between her vagina and anus. She did speak up but was not heard. Reflecting on the experience, Emmy exhibits a split consciousness. Even though she recognized "almost right away" that something was wrong with her body, she remembers thinking, "I'm not going to make waves" (12). Years later in her interview with Sterk, Emmy downplays the doctor's action even as she names it: "I don't want to make a big deal about this but I do think there was malpractice" (12).

In challenging the authority of the medical model, a body-knowing Self assumes its own authority. In her interview, Lee H. (1996, 8) explains: "I do remember [telling the doctor] . . . that we were having pain on intercourse and having the schmuck have the nerve to say to me, 'You probably just can't relax. Maybe try a little glass of wine before you make love.' I remember stalking, at this point I was starting to emerge from that 'there's something wrong with me,' out of his office thinking, 'What the hell does he know? I've been married seven years. We're not talking about I need to relax a little bit. I'm not a nervous bride.'" Maria M. (1996, 5) narrates a comparable encounter in her interview: "[the doctor] was like, 'What a great cut I did to you. See it? You'll be able to wear a bikini again.' At that moment it really hit me. 'This woman cut me open and she's bragging about it?' I just felt something was really wrong with this. I didn't know. I wasn't educated about it. I wasn't totally in touch with how I was feeling because our culture doesn't allow that, 'You should be happy, you have a healthy baby.'" Both women had reached a point where they believed their bodies more than they did their doctors.

Once authority is granted to a body-knowing Self, a woman may gain the confidence to name and to act. Alexandria O. (1996, 12) remembers in her interview how her body knowledge helped her insist on a vaginal birth: "I kept saying, ' . . . I know that this is not supposed to be a c-section. I know that everything's okay, and he's supposed to come out vaginally.' This is before I had the tests [ultrasound and telemetry] done," which proved her body knowledge to be correct. Likewise, Sally D. (1996, 11) recounts in her interview how she shut "external forces out" and "just felt . . . intuitively" that she needed no fetal monitor or IV; what she needed was to get comfortable so that she would be ready for her vbac and not need a c-section. According to Frances B.'s interview (1996, 10), she experienced her body knowledge as a warning voice: "'If you don't stop pulling back, you are going to kill the baby.'" After hearing this voice, she began pushing. With faith in body knowing, women can make themselves heard within the medical model and challenge it in ways that redefine it, their Selves, and their birthing experiences. The results may potentially benefit everyone involved.

STRATEGY #3: CREATING NARRATIVE SPACES FOR THAT-WHICH-IS-NOT-PROPER-TO-DISCUSS

Etiquette dictates what may or may not be said. What is often unsaid is that ideology dictates etiquette. Thus, propriety is more than manners; it is politics. In terms of birthing, propriety is vested in how U.S. culture values the reproductive capacity of women's bodies. Interestingly, a split exists. The reproductive capacity is lauded; the reproducing body, loathed. Stories of motherhood as a cultural good abound; stories of birthing as a bodily process are exiled. The stories of women's bodies that remain in the dominant discourse emerge as erotica. To revise this cultural reduction of the value of women's bodies, we must not only expand existing spaces of propriety for discussing birthing but also give the discussions a new hearing.

A first step is to narrate that-which-is-not-proper-to-discuss and invite it into our dominant discourses. For if that-which-is-not-proper-to-discuss enters popular discourse as common knowledge—or even better, if the whole idea of proper knowledge about women's bodies is called into question—then women and men who experience such issues will feel less alone, less crazy, less guilty. In the United States, birthing is surrounded by a wealth of issues needing expanded spaces and new hearings: infertility, unwed motherhood, fatherhood, adoptions, abortions, miscarriage, prematurity, birth defects, postpartum depression, breastfeeding, and sexuality.[13] Narrating such issues renders visible our birthing socialization and its effects. Narrating the complexity of birthing renders clarity to our decision making.

Precisely because infertility seems unrelated to birthing, it is a perfect issue for exposing our socialization about birthing. Infertility hovers around birthing, often unspoken. Many people perceive infertility as the flip side of birthing, believing giving birth is "normal" and being infertile is "abnormal." In an excellent study of infertility in Massachusetts, Elizabeth Britt (1997, 68) argues that, when the infertile internalize this normal/abnormal socialization, they move into the "infertility closet," where they "may experience a profound sense of alienation from their bodies, families, friends, co-workers, and communities."[14] Within this state of alienation, the infertile must make a host of decisions—whether to accept their "fate," whether to adopt, or whether to employ reproductive technologies.

According to the interviews of Jane E. (1996) and Didi D. (1996), the options of the infertile may also include natural birthing. As an old wives' tale contends, a few infertile couples sometimes need only consider adoption to become pregnant, the idea being of course that once the pressure to conceive is removed, conception becomes possible. Jane E. confirms this tale: "I was just about ready to give up and [my partner] and I were thinking of adoption. . . . Within a year, I had two miscarriages and then became pregnant" (2). Didi D. also confirms this tale: "We had been in the adoption system for about eight months. . . . We went for our first baby 'visit' on Friday and on Monday I went to the doctor and found out I was pregnant" (1). Didi and her husband ended up with two babies, less than a year apart.

Not everyone replicates these experiences, however. Infertility haunts many literary and lived narratives as an absence of birthing. Given infertility's connection with absence (read lack, pain, shame, and grief), it can be a hard story to tell—and to hear. Sometimes the infertile cannot tell their own stories. In Christine Schutt's "Sisters" (1989), the infertile woman's sister narrates the story, in language that assumes birthing to be the norm: "My sister has problems: she is missing some parts and what is there—enough—doesn't quite work as it should, so that now she sees her body as something apart, a shadow, stumped or lengthening depending on the date with one high-noon dissolve when, for a short while, she is all of a piece and the air is moted with possibility" (139). This sister tells the husband's tale too, as it is filtered through his wife, in language that again assumes birthing to be the norm: "She tells me Peter has cried when the shots haven't worked, and sometimes she thinks Peter must regret being saddled with her, a useless, *barren* woman" (142). The narrator also describes her own implication in her sister's infertility: "When I hear about their suffering, I feel helpless, probably in the way Mother said she felt when I told her I was getting a divorce. What can you do?" (142). The point, of course, is twofold: one, the pain of infertility is multifaceted, far-reaching, and inextricably linked to the desire for giving birth; and two, this pain is exacerbated because of cultural discourses that define infertility as abnormal.

Sometimes, however, the infertile tell their own stories. Sharon Thesen's poem "Elegy, The Fertility Specialist" (1989, 144) captures the pain and grief of an infertile woman who leaves her doctor's office after being told she can never conceive: "We make the usual / small gestures of disappointment . . . / And it is / as if something with wings was crushing itself / to my heart, to comfort / or to be comforted I didn't know which." One reason this story is so hard to tell is that the protagonists are mourning the death of the idea of a child. Another reason is that there is no time to recover because monthly rhythms of life serve as constant reminders. For the woman in Gloria Frym's "Strange Fruit" (1989, 151), the reminder is "this monthly blood, still ripping out the heart with a dull knife." As Britt (1997, 77) argues, within the medical model, "charting the menstrual cycle is a technology of normalization," albeit one in which women are subjects as well as objects. What becomes important is the focus of such technologies. If used to help infertile women and men understand their own bodies, so much the better. If used to compare their bodies against a national "average" of those who have given birth, then such technologies often emerge as recipes for failure and self-loathing.

In social conversations, infertile couples often play by the rules of propriety, revealing their situation only via language tropes. The most popular one is silence, which hides the depth of sorrow and pain: "Until she became pregnant, Susan and Paul told only a few people about their infertility experience" (Britt 1997, 85). Infertile couples remain silent for many reasons: fear of jinxing conception, fear of betraying a spouse, fear of public pity or judgment. This silence is made possible, as Britt notes, "[b]ecause infertility is an invisible stigma" (87) that may last a moment, a year, a lifetime. Another trope is understatement, which hides anxiety and hope. Jane E. (1996)—an obstetrician who underwent two donor inseminations, two miscarriages, and "super ovulation with perganol and metrogen" (2) before carrying a child to term—begins her interview with this claim: "I think I have to preface it by saying . . . I had some fertility problems" (1). Alexandria O. (1996, 1) echoes this trope, opening her interview with "I had fertility problems before [conceiving] and I just didn't expect to ever get pregnant."

The consequences of infertility are manifold. Sometimes infertility is temporary (Jane E. 1996; Didi D. 1996; Alexandria O. 1996). Sometimes it is permanent. When permanent, it can strain relationships in ways that shut out all other commonalities among partners, as in Lyn Lifshin's "The Daughter I Don't Have" (1989, 175): "The child we will / not have is all / we wanted, all that / holds us together." It can even end relationships, as in Joyce Carol Oates's "A Touch of Flu" (1989, 176): "For years she tried to conceive a child, and failed; and failed at the marriage too— though 'failed' is probably the wrong word, since wanting a child so badly, and, as some observers (including her husband) said, so irrationally, she simply decided to give up on that man, and move on to another. And so she did; and conceived within months. . . ." For the narrator in Frym's "Strange Fruit" (1989), infertility moves outward: "every pregnant woman is my enemy. It's nothing personal, a certain curve magnetizes my eye. It seems like hatred but it is really sorrow" (145). Infertility moves inward, too: "I begin to grow younger and younger. Wanting the child, I become the child, until I am the child, crying easily and without language" (146). She is without language to express a very real desire that others see only as obsession. For many of the infertile, "[a]ll desire [is] translated into what we could not have" (149).

For the infertile who are unwilling to challenge society's normal/abnormal dichotomy, their options are silence, support groups, or reproductive technologies. For those willing to challenge this dichotomy, there is adoption. Like the narrator in Frym's "Strange Fruit" (1989, 151), the infertile may reimagine their situation as a possibility: "[t]hat I could not hold this one inside, my grief. But that I could take one to be mine to protect, my pleasure. Child who could not be mothered by another, come to me. . . ." Given this focus on possibilities, narrating infertility cannot be done without also narrating reproductive technologies, adoption, unwanted pregnancies, unwed parents, and so on—a circling of events illustrating how inextricably intertwined issues surrounding birthing really are. Narrating such expanded possibilities of what-is-proper-to-discuss about birthing constructs, I believe, a more healthy environment for everyone.

STRATEGY #4: NAMING AND NARRATING THAT-WHICH-IS-NOT-NAMED

Naming is how we "structure the chaos and flux of existence which would otherwise be an undifferentiated mass" (Spender 1980, 163). Because naming "impose[s] a pattern and a meaning which allows us to manipulate the world" (163), it is neither innocent nor neutral but always already implicated in the ideology of those who possess the power to name. That-which-is-not-named, then, is not named because those with power neither acknowledge its existence, value its function, nor trust its compliance if named. In the case of birthing, the result is a socially constructed cultural literacy, presented as a totalizing whole but representing only partial knowledge. This partial knowledge motivated Laura Chester to edit an anthology of birthing literature, *Cradle and All: Women Writers on Pregnancy and Birth,* encompassing the "woes as well as the wonder" of birthing (1989b, 1). Although out of print (another exile of birthing narratives?), Chester's anthology has the right idea in arguing for an expanded, more inclusive repertoire of naming possibilities.

Within U.S. culture, naming is trapped in a system of binary oppositions; everything falling outside the region of "named" is relegated to the region of "no name," quickly becoming "the unknown" and even "the unimaginable." This system of binary oppositions not only poses false options but further falsifies them when we are encouraged to embrace one term or the other: for example, fear/hope, pain/pleasure, cesarean/natural. The medical model embraces the first terms; the nostalgic natural childbirth model, the second. As a result, women are offered the options of either being at the doctor's mercy or being totally in control. Lee H. (1996) articulates the limits of such false options in her interview when she describes her ultrasound experience. After having told the nurse and the doctor that she wanted "minimal exposure," she concluded, "This is a concept that does not occur to them. They have only off/on. You're [either] fine with this or there is something weird about you" (20).

What is often unimaginable within such a binary system is that a third (or fourth) ground exists. A third ground, such as Rohman's modern midwifery model, would enable us to expose false dichotomies like Lee H.'s "fine" or "weird" and to reimagine birth as both "gain" and "loss," "Yes and no," and "Hell and Heaven," as does Rachel Hadas in "Two and One" (1989, 227). A third ground would help us transcend opposing questions—such as, is birthing "measureless pleasure? / Is it measureless pain?" (Ostriker 1989b, 240)—and enable us to say *both* and/or *neither.* A third ground would also offer the possibility that people might experience the terms of the binaries in different ways.

In the past thirty years, progress has been made in naming elements of birthing. A plethora of new terms like *transition* now exist for experiences that women always knew existed, as exemplified by Alice

Hoffman's narrator in *Fortune's Daughter* (1989, 120): "She was in the
darkest time before birth, transition, and even though she didn't know
its name, Lila knew, all of a sudden, that she could not go back." These
new terms have disrupted and redefined popular discourses about
birthing. A case in point: even though the Lamaze method may be criti-
cized for working in service of the medical model, it (along with the
Bradley method) has helped usher birth into more cultural conversations by bringing males into the birthing process as *coaches* (a metaphor
that makes the feminized role of doula acceptable to men) and by developing terms for that-which-has-traditionally-had-no-name, for example,
vaginal rings. Yet women have refused counterintuitive naming, as evidenced by Elise N. (1996, 12) in her interview: "I read a ridiculous piece
by Grantly Dick Reed called 'Childbirth Without Fear' or 'Childbirth
Without Pain' one or the other. . . . Let's not call it pain and if we don't
call it pain, then it isn't." Women have focused instead on naming existing experiences. Sally D. (1996, 13) says in her interview that instead
focusing on whether or not she was in pain, she "focused in on what the
pain was doing."

Yet, there are still thoughts and feelings and states of being that have
no name. For example, still unnamed are possibilities for mother-child
relations outside named, socially sanctioned institutions. Rich (1986)
articulates this issue when writing about one Vermont summer when her
boys were small:

> Without a male adult in the house, without any reason for schedules, naps,
> regular mealtimes, or early bedtimes so the two parents could talk, we fell
> into what I felt to be a delicious and sinful rhythm. It was a spell of unusu-
> ally hot weather . . . ; we lived half-naked, stayed up to watch bats and stars
> and fireflies, read and told stories, slept late. . . . We lived like castaways on
> some island of mothers and children. . . . I remember thinking: This is
> what living with children could be—without school hours, fixed routines,
> naps, the conflict of being both mother and wife with no room for being
> simply myself. (194)

Nikki Giovanni (1989) echoes this conflict in the opening lines of "Don't
Have a Baby till You Read This": "The nurses all said, 'You're fine now,
Mother,' and I said, 'My name is Nikki,' and they said, 'Yes, Mother'"
(105). Here Giovanni is robbed of her identity and given in its place institutional expectations of motherhood. Before such ideas became too

ingrained in herself or her child, she decided "to get [her child] out of there before they got [his] heart" (106).

Atwood pinpoints another unnamed action in "Giving Birth" (1989, 84): "a woman who did not wish to become pregnant, who did not choose to divide herself like this. . . . The word in English for unwanted intercourse is rape. But there is no word in the language for what is about to happen to this woman." There are other things that exist but have no name. As Elise N. (1996) recounts in her interview, she did not know the name for (and hence the existence of) her vaginal ring and, thus, was not able to advocate for a vaginal birth in her first two pregnancies. As Maria M. (1996, 8) says in her interview, she had no language for how stress affects the child in the womb and, thus, was not able to make informed choices about her pregnancy: "I can't change it now but women learn. . . . If there was some kind of stressful thing like that going on, I would just pick up and get myself out of the situation."

The above instances exemplify how more accurate naming can lead to knowledge and control. Women may control birthing experiences, but only if our experiences are accurately named, only if our body knowledge is shared, and only if decisions are enacted based upon this knowledge. By naming the false dichotomies that haunt our lives, women may become more active agents in unbinding our double-binds.

STRATEGY #5: UNBINDING WOMEN'S DOUBLE-BINDS

A consequence of Western binary logic is that it traps women within double-binds. A famous example is the madonna/whore dichotomy, which prohibits our imagining women's bodies as sites of both mother-hood and sexuality. Yet the first term, *madonna*, also has a double-bind implicit within it. As the cultural position of *mother* has evolved in the United States, it has developed two distinct subcategories: the good and the bad. The good mother is the woman who sacrifices all for her chil-dren; the bad mother is the one who does not. The first option forces a woman to subsume her own interests and desires to her family's; the sec-ond option forces her to subsume her family's interests to her own. This either/or logic offers no third term, no middle ground, no balance. As such, it informs not only how society views women but how women view themselves.

Because no one can live up to the ideal of continual self-sacrifice without occasionally having an uncharitable thought or two, all mothers

at one time or another fall into the category of "bad mother." In her interview, Lee H. (1996, 6) describes "bad" this way: "that time of constantly
being on call, constantly having my body at this other person's [s]ervice
was very hard for me." As evidenced in Jane Lazarre's *The Mother Knot*
(1989), "bad" may take many forms. It may manifest itself as selfishness:
"Who was he [the baby] and by what authority had he claimed the right
to my life? (209). It may manifest itself as anxiety:

> I would never be a good mother. Hadn't I already caused him to be colicky
> with my own treacherous anxiety? The experts were right, I thought. Babies
> are born to be placid, contented creatures. It is only the bad mother repress-
> ing her unfair resentment, holding the baby too tightly, too loosely, too
> often, too rarely, letting him cry, picking him up too soon, feeding him too
> much, too little, suffocating him with her love or not loving him enough—
> it is only the bad mother who is to blame. (209)

Sometimes "bad" may manifest itself as hatred: "Sometimes I hated him
for rejecting me so completely; 'Shut up! I'll kill myself if you don't shut
up!' I'd yell. Then I would try to shove my nipple into his mouth and he
would push it away, his face distorted with pain. I'd put him in the car-
riage so as not to harm him with my tentacles of rage, and I'd sit huddled
on the couch, door slammed unsuccessfully against his cries, holding my
ears and moaning with loss . . ." (210). Sometimes "bad" may manifest
itself as anger: "And when he had cried long enough to subdue my anger,
I held him and rocked him again until he became quiet" (210).
Interestingly, "bad" may also manifest itself as loving too much, as evidenced by the very normal mother in Maxine Chernoff's "How Lies
Grow" (1989, 236): "The fourth time I lied to my baby, I told him the
truth, I thought. I told him how he'd have to leave me someday. . . . But
then I thought, I want him to live with me forever. Someday he'll leave
me: then what will I do?" By categorizing all these actions as "bad," society and individual women lose sight of the fact that all of these reactions
are normal, that almost every mother has experienced at least one of
these reactions.

Thus, we need to revise this good/bad dichotomy, recognizing that
negative thoughts do not equal abusive actions and that mistakes are a
part of parenthood. The persona in Ostriker's "Propaganda Poem" (1989c,
27) models this stance, delineating negative thoughts about children without accepting the "bad mother" moniker: "That they limit your liberty, of

course, entirely. / That they limit your cash. That they limit your sleep. / Your sleep is a dirty torn cloth. / That they whine until you want to murder them. / That their beauty prevents you. . . ." Likewise, Lee H. (1996) acknowledges in her interview her gratitude to a La Leche mother who confessed that she had thought about letting her baby roll off the changing table and calling it an accident but that she had, instead, gone right on changing the diaper and caring for her child. Lee H. says, "That's when I realized that I wasn't crazy because I had also internalized that I was supposed to be tremendously competent and loving and never feel angry or upset with the baby" (7).

Such articulations are invaluable in helping mothers, especially new mothers, work through their anger and frustration without feeling crazy or unnatural and without labeling themselves as "bad mothers." Such articulations help mothers arrive at the sanity described in Joyce Carol Oates's "A Touch of Flu" (1989, 176): "And she was happy with her little girl, if not, as she'd anticipated, ecstatic; except of course in bursts of feeling; wayward, unexpected, dazzling, and brief. These are the moments for which we live, she thought. She wondered if anyone had had that thought before her." The answer, of course, is "Yes." And if we would just speak such things, we would know such things. Such knowledge has an impact on more than just a mother's relationship with her child. As Lazarre's new mother concludes with astonishment, "How, I wondered, had I ever blamed my parents for anything?" (1989, 209).

By unbinding double-binds such as the good/bad mother dichotomy, women make spaces for other ways of being in the world—that is, for new plot progressions.

STRATEGY #6: NARRATING NEW PLOTS

Birthing is an old story, perhaps "the oldest we have on our planet" (Olds 1989c, 256). Whatever plot women employ to tell their own birthing narratives, we must take care that it does not repeat the double-binds so common in traditional plotting of women's lives. For example, women may tell birthing narratives by duplicating the classical plot of tragic heroism—that is, separation, initiation, and return to restore the kingdom. The result is a story not about who slayed the most beasts to save the monarch's land but who survived the most pain in order to reaffirm the patriarch's lineage. In *The Mother Daughter Plot*, Marianne Hirsch (1989, 34) argues that, by invoking this plot, women "ally themselves with the 'fathers' and 'brothers' in their own literary tradition." Moreover, if women focus only on the pain then other events in their birthing experiences may be silenced, suborned, and marginalized, including the fact that some women, like Maya Angelou, experience little pain. As she admits in an aside to readers of *I Know Why the Caged Bird Sings* (1993, 245): "I decided that the pain of delivery was overrated." If these and other birthing events are not plotted, then birthing women suffer a lack of knowledge about what to expect. What results is a lack of control over their own birthing experiences and over their own narration of these experiences. Thus, the vicious cycle continues.

This cycling has unfortunate results, especially when mothers and daughters do not talk, as evidenced by Sage B. (1996, 6) in her interview: "I had heard in my birth class that some women have their water break earlier and they really don't go into full labor but usually what happens is that women never get to go into natural labor because labor is induced so they don't have very many stories about these type of women. I later found out that this had happened to my mother but I didn't know then." This example reinforces Hirsch's (1989, 36) claim that in the West mother/daughter narratives progress not via productive dialogue but via "the limiting repetitions and deathly closures of Electra and Antigone." If women's only plot models are the male-identification of the hero's journey, the silence of Sage B.'s mother, the fake baby of Euripides' Electra, and the death of Sophocles' Antigone, then no wonder birthing narratives are scarce. Thus, women must challenge these traditional plots by telling women-centered birthing stories via women-centered plot structures.[15] Such plots make space for voices of birthing women and others not traditionally heard within birthing narratives.[16]

One alternative plot presented by Anne Tyler (1989) in *Breathing Lessons* includes spaces for women to reflect on changes in birthing practices. That women are even telling their birthing stories is revolutionary, at least according to Maggie, the middle-aged protagonist:

. . ."Breathing lessons—really," [Maggie's daughter-in-law Fiona] said, dropping to the floor with a thud. "Don't they reckon I must know how to breathe by now"?

"Oh, honey, you're just lucky they offer such things. . . . My first pregnancy, there wasn't a course to be found, and I was scared to death. I'd have loved to take lessons! And afterward: I remember leaving the hospital with Jesse and thinking, 'Wait. Are they going to let me just walk off with him?

I don't know beans about babies! I don't have a license to do this. Ira and I are just amateurs.' I mean you're given years and years of lessons in how to balance equations, which Lord knows you will never have to do in normal life. But how about parenthood? Or marriage, either, come to think of it. Before you can drive a car you need a state-approved course of instruction, but driving a car is nothing, nothing, compared to living day in and day out with a husband and raising up a new human being." (38–39)

Breathing lessons signify not just the preparation for labor and delivery that makes birthing more visible in U.S. culture. They also signify a way of life—a revised narrative plot for women wherein we do not have to hold our breath in shame, fearing that we will speak a taboo, fearing that we will do something wrong because we have not been told and cannot ask.

Another alternative plot emerges, according to Hirsch (1989), in revisions of heterosexual romance and marriage storylines.[17] As romance and marriage plots are questioned, spaces emerge for plotting new stories of mother and child. Traditional mother/child plots in the United States (and their double-binds) are described by Emmy B. (1996, 7) in her interview: when she had her children, "there were pressures on young women to choose. It was one or another." Although she adores her children, she readily acknowledges the unspoken, disconcerting undercurrents of being a "full-time mommy": feeling isolated, being at the beck and call of a baby, and fearing to compete career-wise with a husband (8). However this traditional career/motherhood plot has been reimagined. In "35/10" Sharon Olds (1989c) offers "the story of replacement" (256), not a violent replacement, as in the Oedipal myth, but a loving replacement, as in the shared moments of a parent and child, for example, a mother brushing her child's "tangled / fragrant hair at bedtime" (256). Olds's replacement plot preserves family connections without demanding the mother's constant presence or her eventual rejection.

Finally, the heroic journey of separation, initiation, and return may be replaced by birthing women's journey from knowledge to authority to control to celebration. While this new plot should not be imagined as a grand narrative (remember: not all birthing experiences culminate in happily-ever-after endings), this new plot is important. For, according to Lee H. (1996, 26) in her interview, birthing women need *knowledge* about childbirth because U.S. culture "is structured to disempower you, to have you feel weak and inadequate." According to Sally D. (1996), knowledge offers birthing women a sense of *authority,* of knowing what to expect and how to handle it. This authority engenders a much-needed *control,* for as Lee H. (1996, 12) asserts, "it's not the pain that gets to you, it's the lack of control." And in most (but not all)[18] cases, control generates a sense of *celebration,* of accomplishment, as evidenced in Sharon Olds's (1989a, 135) "The Language of the Brag":

> I have done what you wanted to do, Walt Whitman,
> Allen Ginsberg, I have done this thing,
> I and the other women this exceptional
> act with the exceptional heroic body,
> this giving birth, this glistening verb,
> and I am putting my proud American boast
> right here with the others.

Though Olds may be foregrounding the physical act of giving birth, this poem also captures the emotional act of giving birth, an act available to mothers and fathers, both biological and adopted.

BEGINNINGS

In *The Pink Guitar,* Rachel DuPlessis (1990, 161) poses seemingly intriguing questions: "If we had a non-patriarchal symbolic order, what would the language be in that situation? What would the non-patriarchal 'word' be?" If we apply these questions to birthing narratives, we, too, would have seemingly intriguing questions. Yet such questions hover on the brink of idealism, threatening to sever connections with material reality. And our material reality is this: we *do* have a patriarchal symbolic order, a language system suspicious of women's experiences. We cannot step outside of this symbolic order; we can only revise it from within. Consequently, one response to DuPlessis's questions is to circle through the questions posed in this study—(1) What strategies un/consciously exile women's birthing narratives from our dominant discourses? and (2) What strategies challenge this exile? Internalizing these questions may help us to recognize such strategies when they occur in our lives and to re/act accordingly. In my own life, I research and teach women's literary and lived birthing narratives and their strategies in hopes of creating a space for them not only within academic discourses but also within students' lives. In turn, I hope these stories help us all rethink our gender socialization about birthing in ways that give birthing women more control of, and everyone else more respect for, one of the oldest stories on the planet.[19]

NOTES

1. Mill (1974) is focusing on all of women's experiences, not solely birthing narratives, and he is focusing on the United Kingdom, not the United States, but Brown et al. (1994) argue that this quotation also explains birthing in the United States.

2. When I use the term "U.S. culture," I am referring to the dominant U.S. culture as it is influenced by Western thinking. Although multiple cultures coexist in the United States, we are all socialized, in different ways, by this dominant culture.

3. Other myths include (1) Lamaze courses, which present childbirth as a sporting event, complete with its own "rules of the game" that, if learned and faithfully practiced, promise control over labors and deliveries; (2) a paucity of breast-feeding information, which leads women to believe that breast milk magically appears and disappears; (3) gender socialization, which prevents our imagining women as both mothers and sexual beings (Chester 1989f; Huggan 1989; Kahn 1995); and (4) medical ideology, which convinces people that they need the expert knowledge and delivery skills of doctors as well as accompanying technology, obscuring the fact that, during routine births, our doctors are present for only the final few moments, while our nurses stay with us for hours.

4. Rothman (1982) offers extended definitions of the medical model and the midwifery model. The medical model promotes the ideology of technology (the body as a machine that needs repair), an assumption that the male body is the norm and the female body is a complication of the norm, and a definition of natural childbirth that includes intrusive procedures such as fetal monitoring, drugs, forceps, episiotomies, and the like. The midwifery model promotes a holistic ideology (mind/spirit/body connections), an assumption that the female body is the norm, and a definition of natural childbirth that includes birthing women and midwives reading each birthing woman's body to determine its needs and then proceeding nonintrusively.

5. To define *narrative*, Hodge (1990) traces its etymologies to the Latin *narrare*, to tell a story, and to *gnarus*, which means knowledgeable about. He then argues that narrative "retains this potent like between knowing and telling which is central to its ideological effectiveness, since it seems to guarantee a transparent form of telling in which the form of speech closely matches its object. This object is itself regarded as transparent, taken-for-granted concrete world of actions, processes and events, along with the patterns of causality and linkages that make sense of it" (173). He claims that literature categorizes narrative as "novels, short stories, and narrative poems" (175) and that Lévi-Strauss adds myth, one of which is childbirth.

6. Simkin (1991, 1992, and 1996) claims that women accurately remember their birthing events and feelings for at least twenty years after their deliveries. Githens et al. (1993) found 89 percent agreement between women's medical records and their recall; the recall data was gathered via phone interviews 5.7 years (on average) after the women's deliveries.

7. To explore problems associated with this move, see Singley and Sweeney (1993).

8. For a critique of the childbirth metaphor in relation to the creative process of the poet H.D., see Hollenberg (1991); for a rejection of the cultural split between writing and motherhood, see Walker (1983). I am indebted to my colleague Ed Duffy for suggesting the Aeschylus selections.

9. Mary Daly (1990) has revised the Athena myth. By nicknaming Athena "Daddy's girl" (8), Daly foregrounds Athena's patriarchal identification. By imagining a "thrice-born Athena"—born not just of her mother's womb, not just of her father's brow, but of her own language and experience—Daly encourages Athena to give birth to a new self, one possessed of a woman-centered consciousness and one that acknowledges her African roots in the goddess Neith. This thrice-born Athena serves as a role model for all of us, exemplifying the power we possess to give birth to new selves.

10. I am indebted to my colleague, Amelia Sandy, for suggesting this birthing scene.

11. Re/definitions of *birth* as *love* haunt literature. See Jaffe 1989a, Schwartz 1989, Olds 1989b, and Gingher 1989.

12. Rich (1986) connects this reimagined ground to a reimagined sense of female biology:

> Patriarchal thought has limited female biology to its own narrow specifications. The feminist vision has recoiled from female biology for these reasons [i.e., the traps of essentialism]; it will, I believe, come to view our physicality as a resource, rather than a destiny. In order to live a fully human life we require not only *control* of our bodies (though control is a prerequisite); we must touch the unity and resonance of our physicality, our bond with the natural order, the corporeal ground of our intelligence. (40)

13. For literary representations of issues that affect birthing, see the following: unwed motherhood and fatherhood (Derricotte 1989), adoptions (Gingher 1989; Hoffman 1989), abortions (Bergé 1989; Brenner 1989b; Brooks 1993; Castillo 1992; Sexton 1993), miscarriage (Huggan 1989), stillbirth (Chester 1989e; Nin 1989), prematurity and birth defects (Mørch 1989), postpartum depression (Emmy B. 1996; Oates 1989; Sage B. 1996), breastfeeding (Emmy B. 1996; Frances B. 1996; Harris 1989; Lee H. 1996; Ostriker 1989a), and the sexuality of birthing (Chester 1989f; Huggan 1989; Kahn 1995; Mørch 1989; Thompson 1989).

14. Britt (1997) defines *normal* and *abnormal:*

> "normal" fertility does not mean that all couples will conceive every time they try. For a practitioner of infertility medicine, "normal" fertility means that a couple (based on an average age of twenty-five) has a 20 percent chance of conceiving in any given cycle (Tan and Seibel, 30). In addition, because fertility is a continuum rather than a binary, some individuals within a population will never be able to conceive. In other words, it is "normal" for a certain number of people within a population to be unable to conceive. For the individual or couple, however, being normal means being able to have a child. (94)

For the record, Britt claims that medical and legal definitions "place the boundary between normal and abnormal fertility at one year" (75).

15. One alternative plot structure, offered by Hirsch (1989), is the Persephone/Demeter myth. It unfolds not through an Aristotelian beginning, middle, and end but through continued *"opposition, interruption, and contradiction"* (35). Hirsch finds herself relying on Greek myths because of their ongoing influence: "I find not only that certain familial and narrative patterns do tend to predominate and to continue to inform modern writing, but also that they help to explain how, on the one hand, female difference is inscribed and attempted, and how, on the other, it can easily be subverted by a repetition of the same" (29). Still, she acknowledges that these myths are "seriously insufficient as paradigms for female and feminist plotting" (29).

16. Voices of birthing women are discussed in Hindmarch (1989), Howe, (1989), Lee H. (1996), O'Brien (1989), and Phillips (1989); voices of others attending the birthing are discussed in Chester (1989d) and Lee H. (1996).

17. Hirsch (1989) notes the historical development of these storylines: "in the nineteenth century the plot of the heterosexual romance and marriage structures the novels of women writers, even if its conventional sequence is variously subverted" (9); in the 1920s women writers began downplaying plots of heterosexual love and the romance and celebrating stories about mothers (96). According to Hirsch, Susan Gubar attributes this shift from romance to motherhood to improved technology and changing social conditions: "in [Gubar's] excellent discussion of the female *Künstlerroman*, the invention, improvement, and greater availability of contraception, the radically lower birth rate, and the significant decrease in mother and infant mortality . . . made it possible for women writers to reimagine the maternal" (97).

18. An example of a birth not celebrated occurs in Tan's *Joy Luck Club* (1989, 116–17).

19. Other sources of literary and lived birthing narratives include: Dwinell (1992), Pollock (1999), Richards (1987), and Silko (1990). Scholarly analyses of birthing narratives include: Benjamin (1993), who offers a collection that investigates how science and birthing are intertwined; Lindenbaum and Lock (1993), who offer a comparative analysis of lived birthing stories from around the world; and Magee (1999), who offers a study of birthing in southern women's fiction. Internet sources of birthing narratives include the following sites: *Labor of love* (1997), Kurokawa (n.d.), Matthew (1999), and Plomp (1998).

REFERENCES

Aeschylus. 1975. *The oresteia*. Translated by Robert Fagles. New York: Penguin Classics, Viking.

Alexandria O. 1996. Interview by Helen Sterk, 28 May. Available from Memorial Library Archives, Marquette University, Milwaukee, WI 53201.

Angelou, M. 1993. *I know why the caged bird sings*. New York: Bantam Books. Original edition New York: Random House, 1970.

Atwood, M. 1989. Giving birth. In *Cradle and all: Women writers on pregnancy and birth*, ed. L. Chester, 80–91. Boston: Faber & Faber. Reprinted from *Dancing girls*, New York: Simon & Schuster, 1977.

Benjamin, Marina, ed. 1993. *A question of identity: Women, science, and literature.* New Brunswick, N.J.: Rutgers University Press.

Bergé, C. 1989. Extract from *Acts of love: An American novel.* In *Cradle and all,*
ed. L. Chester, 182–85. Boston: Faber & Faber. Reprinted from *Acts of
love,* Indianapolis: Bobbs-Merrill, 1974.

Brenner, S. 1989a. Blissed raga. In *Cradle and all,* ed. L. Chester, 40–41.
Boston: Faber & Faber. Reprinted from *From the heart to the center,*
Berkeley, Calif.: The Figures, 1977.

———. 1989b. Inches and lives. In *Cradle and all,* ed. L. Chester, 186–87.
Boston: Faber & Faber. Reprinted from *The soft room,* Berkeley, Calif.: The
Figures, 1978.

Britt, E. 1997. Conceiving the American dream: Ethnographic interpretations
of law, rhetoric, and infertility. Ph.D. diss., Rensselaer Polytechnic
Institute, Troy, N.Y.

Brooks, G. 1993. The mother. In *No more masks: An anthology of twentieth-cen-
tury American women poets,* ed. F. Howe, 95–96. New York: HarperCollins.
Reprinted from *The world of Gwendolyn Brooks,* New York: Harper and
Row Publishers, 1960.

Brown, S., J. Lumley, R. Small, and J. Astbury. 1994. *Missing voices: The experience of motherhood.* Melbourne, Australia: Oxford University Press.

Butler, J. 1993. *Bodies that matter: On the discursive limits of "sex."* New York:
Routledge.

Castillo, A. 1992. *The Mixquiahuala Letters.* New York: Doubleday. Original
edition 1986.

Chernoff, M. 1989. How lies grow. In *Cradle and all,* ed. L. Chester, 236.
Boston: Faber & Faber. Reprinted from *American poetry since 1970: Up late,*
edited by A. Codrescu, New York: Four Walls Eight Windows, 1988.

Chester, L., ed. 1989a. *Cradle and all: Women writers on pregnancy and birth.*
Boston: Faber & Faber.

———. 1989b. Introduction. In *Cradle and all,* ed. L. Chester, 1–4. Boston:
Faber & Faber.

———. 1989c. Extract from *Primagravida.* In *Cradle and all,* ed. L. Chester,
203. Boston: Faber & Faber. Reprinted from *Primagravida,* Santa Barbara,
Calif.: Christopher's Books, 1975.

———. 1989d. Song of being born. In *Cradle and all,* ed. L. Chester, 77.
Boston: Faber & Faber. Reprinted from *Primagravida,* Santa Barbara,
Calif.: Christopher's Books, 1975.

———. 1989e. Extract from *The stone baby.* In *Cradle and all,* ed. L. Chester,
126–29, 189–90. Boston: Faber & Faber. Reprinted from *The stone baby,*
Santa Rosa, Calif.: Black Sparrow Press, 1989.

————. 1989f. Suckle sex. In *Cradle and all*, ed. L. Chester, 49. Boston: Faber & Faber. Reprinted from *Primagravida*, Santa Barbara, Calif.: Christopher's Books, 1975.

Colwin, L. 1989. Extract from *Another marvelous thing*. In *Cradle and all*, ed L. Chester, 116–17. Boston: Faber & Faber. Reprinted from *Another marvelous thing*, New York: Alfred A. Knopf, 1982.

Cosslett, T. 1994. *Women writing childbirth: Modern discourses of motherhood*. New York: Manchester University Press.

Crow Dog, M., and R. Erdoes. 1990. *Lakota woman*. New York: HarperPerennial.

Daly, M. 1990. *Gyn/ecology: The metaethics of radical feminism*. 2d ed. Boston: Beacon Press.

Derricotte, T. 1989. Extract from *Natural birth*. In *Cradle and all*, ed. L. Chester, 108–15. Boston: Faber & Faber. Reprinted from *Natural birth*, Trumansburg, N.Y.: Crossing Press, 1983.

Didi D. 1996. Interview by Helen Sterk, 25 June. Available from Memorial Library Archives, Marquette University, Milwaukee, WI 53201.

DuBois, P. 1988. *Sowing the body: Psychoanalysis and ancient representations of women*. Chicago: University of Chicago Press.

DuPlessis, R. 1985. *Writing beyond the ending: Narrative strategies of twentieth-century women writers*. Bloomington: Indiana University Press.

————. 1990. *The pink guitar: Writing as feminist practice*. New York: Routledge.

Dwinell, J. 1992. *Birth stories: Mystery, power, and creation*. Westport, Conn.: Bergin & Garvey.

Eisenberg, A., H. Murkoff, and S. Hathaway. 1991. *What to expect when you're expecting*. 2d ed. New York: Workman Publishers.

Elise N. 1996. Interview by Helen Sterk, n.d. Available from Memorial Library Archives, Marquette University, Milwaukee, WI 53201.

Emmy B. 1996. Interview by Helen Sterk, 7 May. Available from Memorial Library Archives, Marquette University, Milwaukee, WI 53201.

Frances B. 1996. Interview by Helen Sterk, 12 April. Available from Memorial Library Archives, Marquette University, Milwaukee, WI 53201.

Friedman, S. S. 1987. Creativity and the childbirth metaphor: Gender differences in literary discourses. *Feminist Studies* 13:49–82.

Frym, G. 1989. Strange Fruit. In *Cradle and all*, ed. L. Chester, 145–51. Boston: Faber & Faber.

Gayley, C. M. 1939. *The classic myths in English literature and art*. New York: John Wiley & Sons.

Gingher, M. 1989. Camouflage. In *Cradle and all*, ed. L. Chester, 158–74. Boston: Faber & Faber. Reprinted from *Teen angel and other stories of young love*. New York: Atheneum Publishers, 1988.

Giovanni, N. 1989. Don't have a baby till you read this. In *Cradle and all*, ed. L. Chester, 105–6. Boston: Faber & Faber. Reprinted from *Gemini*. New York: Macmillan, 1971.

Githens, P. B., C. A. Glass, F. A. Sloan, and S. S. Entman. 1993. Maternal recall and medical records: An examination of events during pregnancy, childbirth, and early infancy. *Birth* 20:136–41.

Hadas, R. 1989. Two and one. In *Cradle and all*, ed. L. Chester, 227–29. Boston: Faber & Faber. Reprinted from *A son from sleep*. Middletown, Conn.: Wesleyan University Press, 1987.

Harris, M. 1989. Milk. In *Cradle and all*, ed. L. Chester, 198. Boston: Faber & Faber. Reprinted from *Interstate*. Pittsburgh: Slow Loris Press, 1980.

Hindmarch, G. 1989. Extract from *A birth account*. In *Cradle and all*, ed. L. Chester, 63–64. Boston: Faber & Faber. Reprinted from *A birth account*. Vancouver: New Star Books, 1976.

Hirsch, M. 1989. *The mother daughter plot: Narrative, psychoanalysis, feminism*. Bloomington: Indiana University Press.

Hodge, R. 1990. *Literature as discourse*. Baltimore: Johns Hopkins University Press.

Hoffman, A. 1989. Extract from *Fortune's daughter*. In *Cradle and all*, ed. L. Chester, 119–23. Boston: Faber & Faber. Reprinted from *Fortune's daughter*. New York: Putnam, 1985.

Hollenberg, D. K. 1991. *H.D.: The poetics of childbirth and creativity*. Boston: Northeastern University Press.

Howe, F. 1989. Onset. In *Cradle and all*, ed. L. Chester, 16–20. Boston: Faber & Faber.

Huggan, I. 1989. The violation. In *Cradle and all*, ed. L. Chester, 42–48. Boston: Faber & Faber. Original work published 1988.

Jaffe, S. 1989a. The baby laughs. In *Cradle and all*, ed. L. Chester, 7. Boston: Faber & Faber. Reprinted from *The unexamined wife*. Santa Rosa, Calif.: Black Sparrow Press, 1983.

Jaffe, S. 1989b. Something larger. In *Cradle and all*, ed. L. Chester, 260. Boston: Faber & Faber. Reprinted from *The faces that reappear*. Santa Rosa, Calif.: Black Sparrow Press, 1988.

Jaggar, A.R., and S. R. Bordo, eds. 1989. *Gender/body/knowledge: Feminist reconstructions of being and knowing*. New Brunswick, N.J.: Rutgers University Press.

Jane E. 1996. Interview by Helen Sterk, 6 May. Available from Memorial Library Archives, Marquette University, Milwaukee, WI 53201.

Jong, E. 1989. On the first night. In *Cradle and all*, ed. L. Chester, 124–25. Boston: Faber & Faber. Reprinted from *Ordinary miracles*. New York: NAL Penguin, 1983.

Kahn, R. P. 1995. *Bearing meaning: The language of birth*. Urbana: University of Illinois Press.

Karina K. 1996. Interview by Helen Sterk, April. Available from Memorial Library Archives, Marquette University, Milwaukee, WI 53201.

Kurokawa, J. D. n.d. *The coyote midwife home page*. [Online]. Available: http://www.midrivers.com/~jkuro/ [3 March 2000]

1997. *The labor of love*. [Online]. Available: http://www.thelaboroflove.com/ [20 October 2001].

Lazarre, J. 1989. Extract from *The mother knot*. In *Cradle and all*, ed. L. Chester, 209–10. Boston: Faber & Faber. Reprinted from *The mother knot*. New York: McGraw Hill, 1976.

Lee H. 1996. Interview by Helen Sterk, 23 May. Available from Memorial Library Archives, Marquette University, Milwaukee, WI 53201.

Lifshin, L. 1989. The daughter i don't have. In *Cradle and all*, ed. L. Chester, 175. Boston: Faber & Faber.

Lindenbaum, S., and M. Lock, eds. 1993. *Knowledge, power, and practice: The anthropology of medicine and everyday life*. Berkeley: University of California Press.

Magee, R. M. 1999. From grandmother to mother to me: Birth narratives and tradition in the fiction of southern women. In *Southern mothers: Fact and fictions in southern women's writing*, ed. N. Warren and S. Wolff. Baton Rouge: Louisiana State University Press.

Maria M. 1996. Interview by Helen Sterk, 10 May. Available from Memorial Library Archives, Marquette University, Milwaukee, WI 53201.

Marrone, R. L. 1990. *Body of knowledge: An introduction to body/mind psychology*. Albany: State University of New York Press.

Matthew, P. 1999. *Home Birth Families*. [Online]. Available: http://www.home-birthfamilies.com [3 March 2000].

Mill, J. S. 1974. The subjection of women. In *On liberty, representative government, the subjection of women*. London: Oxford University Press. Original works published 1859, 1861, and 1869, respectively.

Molly S. 1996. Interview by Helen Sterk, 7 May. Available from Memorial Library Archives, Marquette University, Milwaukee, WI 53201.

Moore, G. 1983. *Esther Waters*. New York: Oxford University Press. Original work published 1894.

Mørch, D. T. 1989. Extract from *Winter's child*, trans. J. Tate. In *Cradle and all*, ed. L. Chester, 177–81. Boston: Faber & Faber. Original work published 1976.

Morrison, T. 1988. *Beloved*. New York: Plume.

Mossman, C. A. 1993. *Politics and narratives of birth: Gynocolonization from Rousseau to Zola*. New York: Cambridge University Press.

Nin, A. Birth. 1989. In *Cradle and all*, ed. L. Chester, 152–55. Boston: Faber & Faber. Reprinted from *Under a glass bell*. New York: Swallow Press, 1948.

Oates, J. C. 1989. A touch of flu. In *Cradle and all*, ed. L. Chester, 176. Boston: Faber & Faber. Reprinted from *The assignation*. New York: Ecco Press, 1988.

O'Brien, E. 1989. Extract from *The country girls trilogy*. In *Cradle and all*, ed. L. Chester, 54–62. Boston: Faber & Faber. Reprinted from *The country girls trilogy*. New York: Farrar, Straus & Giroux, 1960, 1962, 1964.

Olds, S. 1989a. The language of the brag. In *Cradle and all*, ed. L. Chester, 134–35. Boston: Faber & Faber. Reprinted from *Satan says*. Pittsburgh: University of Pittsburgh Press, 1980.

———. 1989b. The planned child. In *Cradle and all*, ed. L. Chester, 11. Boston: Faber & Faber. Reprinted from *Poetry*, 1985.

———. 1989c. 35/10. In *Cradle and all*, ed. L. Chester, 256. Boston: Faber & Faber. Reprinted from *The dead and the living*. New York: Alfred A. Knopf, 1983.

Ostriker, A. 1989a. Letter to m. In *Cradle and all*, ed. L. Chester, 211. Boston: Faber & Faber. Reprinted from *The mother/child papers*. Boston: Beacon Press, 1980.

———. 1989b. Mother/child. In *Cradle and all*, ed. L. Chester, 240. Boston: Faber & Faber. Reprinted from *The mother/child papers*. Boston: Beacon Press, 1980.

———. 1989c. Propaganda poem: Maybe for some young mamas. In *Cradle and all*, ed. L. Chester, 25–28. Boston: Faber & Faber. Reprinted from *The mother/child papers*. Boston: Beacon Press, 1980.

Phelan, J. 1996. *Narrative as rhetoric: Technique, audiences, ethics, ideology*. Columbus: Ohio State University Press.

Phillips, J. A. 1989. Bluegill. In *Cradle and all*, ed. L. Chester, 29–34. Boston: Faber & Faber. Reprinted from *Fastlanes*. New York: Penguin Books, 1987.

Plato. 1977. *Phaedrus*, translated by H. N. Fowler. Loeb Classical Library. Cambridge: Harvard University Press, 1:405–579.

Plomp, K. 1998. *Birth stories!!!*. [Online]. Available: http://www.geocities.com/Heartland/7269/ [3 March 2000].

Pollock, D. 1999. *Telling bodies performing birth: Everyday narratives of childbirth.* New York: Columbia University Press.

Rich, A. 1986. *Of woman born: Motherhood as experience and institution.* 2d ed. New York: W.W. Norton. Original work published 1975.

Richards, L. B. 1987. *The vaginal birth after cesarean experience: Birth stories by parents and professionals.* South Hadley, Mass.: Bergin & Garvey.

Rothman, B. K. 1982. *In labor: Women and power in the birthplace.* New York: W.W. Norton.

Sage B. 1996. Interview by Helen Sterk, 10 May. Available from Memorial Library Archives, Marquette University, Milwaukee, WI 53201.

Sally D. 1996. Interview by Helen Sterk, 29 May. Available from Memorial Library Archives, Marquette University, Milwaukee, WI 53201.

Sarah Jane C. 1996. Interview by Helen Sterk, 6 May. Available from Memorial Library Archives, Marquette University, Milwaukee, WI 53201.

Schutt, C. 1989. Sisters. In *Cradle and all,* ed. L. Chester, 139–43. Boston: Faber & Faber.

Schwartz, L. S. 1989. Extract from *Rough strife.* In *Cradle and all,* ed. L. Chester, 13–15. Boston: Faber & Faber. Reprinted from *Rough strife.* New York: Harper & Row, 1980.

Sexton, A. 1993. The abortion. In *No more masks: An anthology of twentieth-century American women poets,* ed. F. Howe, 192. New York: HarperCollins. Reprinted from *All my pretty ones.* New York: Houghton Mifflin, 1962.

Silko, L. M. 1990. Giving birth. In *We are the stories we tell: The best short stories by North American women,* ed. W. Martin. New York: Pantheon Books.

Simkin, P. 1991. Just another day in a woman's life? Part 1. Women's long-term perceptions of their first birth experiences. *Birth: Issues in Perinatal Care* 18:203–10.

———. 1992. Just another day in a woman's life? Part 2. Nature and consistency of women's long-term memories of their first birth experiences. *Birth: Issues in Perinatal Care* 19:64–81.

———. 1996. The experience of maternity in a woman's life. *JOGNN* 25:247–52.

Singley, C. J., and S. E. Sweeney, eds. 1993. *Anxious power: Reading, writing, and ambivalence in narrative by women.* Albany: State University of New York Press.

Smith, J. C. 1996. *The castration of Oedipus: Feminism, psychoanalysis, and the will to power.* New York: New York University Press.

Sorri, M. 1989. *A post-modern epistemology: Language, truth, and body.* Lewiston, N.Y.: E. Mellen Press.

Spender, D. 1980. *Man made language.* New York: Routledge.

————. 1989. *The writing or the sex? or why you don't have to read women's writing to know it's no good.* New York: Pergamon Press.

Tan, A. 1989. *The joy luck club.* New York: Ivy Books.

Thesen, S. 1989. Elegy, the fertility specialist. In *Cradle and all,* ed. L. Chester, 144. Boston: Faber & Faber.

Thompson, J. 1989. Dreams of a new mother. In *Cradle and all,* ed. L. Chester, 200–202. Boston: Faber & Faber. Reprinted from *East is west of here.* Portland, Ore.: Breitenbush Books, 1987.

Tolstoy, L. 1952. *War and peace.* Edited by R. M. Hutchins, translated by L. and A. Maude. Great Books of the Western World, vol. 51. Chicago: Encyclopedia Britannica, Inc. Original work published 1863.

Travis, M. 1998. *Reading cultures: The construction of readers in the twentieth century.* Carbondale: Southern Illinois University Press.

Tyler, A. 1989. Extract from *Breathing lessons.* In *Cradle and all,* ed. L. Chester, 38–39. Boston: Faber & Faber. Reprinted from *Breathing lessons.* New York: Alfred A. Knopf, 1988.

Walker, A. 1983. A writer because of, not in spite of, her children. In *In search of our mothers' gardens,* 66–70. London: Women's Press.

3

COMMUNICATION, CARE, AND CONTROL

A Communication Perspective

Helen M. Sterk

$\mathcal{A}$ dutiful Armed Forces wife of the 1950s, Mimi W. had endured two army hospital births. She had been treated brusquely by doctors and was warehoused in a ward that held more than fifty other women. Since there were few nurses, Mimi and the other women had to care for their own sanitary needs. To get to their newborns, Mimi and the other women had to walk up a flight of stairs. Once there, they nursed their babies under the watchful eyes of the men painting the nursing room. The entire experience felt shameful and humiliating to Mimi.

For Mimi's third birth, she chose what she called a "celebrity doctor," a city doctor known for white glove treatment of his clients. Since he conducted births on Thursdays, she entered the hospital on Wednesday night and, after a dinner out with her husband, Mimi received a shot to put her to sleep. In the morning, she woke with an itchy rash. Soon after the nurse gave Mimi another shot to counteract the rash, Mimi sank into unconsciousness. Later that day, she says, "When I woke up, I was in this beautiful pink room, soft music was playing. I looked over and my husband was in the room. I thought, 'Oh boy, I'm going back to sleep. This baby isn't even born yet.' I didn't want to feel this like I did the other one, so I was going to just try and nod off again. My husband saw that I had awakened and he said, 'We have a beautiful baby girl.' I said, 'We do?' I was totally surprised that we had this baby" (Mimi W. 1996, 16). Mimi's tailbone and throat hurt. Later, she discovered the doctor had broken her tailbone in order to pull the baby out and that an oxygen tube had been forced down her throat during labor and delivery.

Mimi's experience differs mainly in intensity, rather than in kind, from the experiences cited in the interviews collected in the Birthing Project. The women's words reveal a communication culture of control, rather than care, that infuses the experience of giving birth in American hospitals. In the case of birthing, a culture of control assumes women do not know themselves and the needs of their babies well enough to make informed decisions about their own care. So, the medical personnel tend to relieve women of decision making and to pacify women by making them "comfortable" during birthing through the use of drugs and decorative settings.

Many of the interviews in the Birthing Project highlight the contrast between care and control as it was experienced by laboring and birthing women. Women whose expectations were met tended to feel cared for, while women who felt they were not listened to and not considered with respect during labor and delivery felt as if they had been controlled.

Nursing, midwifing, and doctoring all entail caring for people. In the context of birthing, two paradigms seem to be in contest for the best way to manage birthing: the one a scientific, observation-based model and the other a humanistic, experience-based model. Many researchers in the areas of nursing and birthing have called for reconsideration of scientific privilege (among them, Hagell 1989; Jordan 1983; Katz Rothman [1982] 1991; Kennedy 1995; McCool and McCool 1989; Sterk and Sterk 1993; Sterk 1996; and Vosler and Burst 1993), arguing that understanding what constitutes good care depends upon access to personal, experiential knowledge. Indeed, Hagell goes so far as to assert that "as nurses become more and more scientific, they will lose what is essential to nursing, i.e., caring itself, because science cannot conceptualize caring nor can caring be measured, only experienced" (1989, 231). Hagell and others realize what communication scholars have known for a long time, that humans construct meaning out of their experiences. In order to find out what something means, you must search for answers among the people who have experienced it.

A key question in any analysis of communication and care is "What counts as care?" The scientific answer might be, "Whatever is determined to best serve the needs of the receiver is caring." The humanistic answer might be, "Care is whatever treatment is understood as satisfactory by the person receiving it." The first answer privileges the point of view of an expert observer, while the second highlights the perspective of the recipient of care. The first encourages caregivers to adopt a paternalistic attitude toward recipients, while the second suggests caregivers see themselves as partners with recipients. Ultimately, this is a good test for quality of care: Is the care seen as such by the person receiving it? If not, then real care has not been given.

Several promising ideas on the pragmatics of care are being developed in communication studies and philosophy. Their promise lies in the ways these ideas help us to create a sense of human respect and to honor our interdependence. Three framing questions include: What is necessary to the idea of care? How might care be expressed and experienced? And how might an ethic of care guide decision making during the period of caring?

WHAT IS CARE?

Through sound association and word play, care prompts consideration of a number of related concepts, such as the Latin term, "cura personalis" (meaning care for the whole person), cure (suggesting a diagnostic potential), curiosity (suggesting an attitude toward persons and situations), curate (an assistant to a parish priest, especially one who serves a divided parish), and curator (a person charged with taking care of something valuable). Each association reinforces an attitude of connection, a recognition of human interdependence, and an acknowledgement of the need to give and receive care.

Care theorists locate the motive to care in a desire for human survival and success. Nel Noddings, author of *Caring: A Feminine Approach to Ethics and Moral Education* (1984), looks to her own experiences and consciousness for evidence of the radical reality of connection. Sara Ruddick, in *Maternal Thinking* (1989), sees care as triggered through caregiving. If you have to take care of someone, you will learn the value of care. Joan Tronto's *Moral Boundaries: A Political Argument for an Ethic of Care* (1993) finds dependency "a natural part of the human experience, one to be accepted rather than seen as 'character destroying'" (163). Caring is framed as part of the human condition, necessary for a good life.

Till now, it virtually has been taken for granted that the purpose of communication is to guide and control behavior, not necessarily to engage in caregiving. Especially in cases where an audience's good (health, safety, and so on) is at stake, the presumption has been that a knowledgeable communicator should persuade an audience to do what is best, as the communicator sees it. Cindy Griffin (1996) frames this presumption as the central, biologically essentialist view of symbolic dynamics that grounds much of the communication studies discipline. Suggesting that male alienation from the reproductive forces of life has driven the construction of a symbolic world in which control, mastery, and artificiality replace flow, connection, and natural methods, Griffin urges consideration of symbolic constructs that originate in ideas of connection rather than separation. Other scholars attuned to the possibilities of communication that cares rather than controls encourage active consideration of what such communication looks like, sounds like, and acts like (Blair, Brown, and Baxter 1994; Foss and Griffin 1992, 1995; Sterk and Turner 1994; Sullivan and Goldzwig 1995; Wood 1992, 1994).

The voice speaking most distinctly about the value of care as a core communication principle belongs to Julia Wood. According to Wood (1994), all humans "live embodied lives, constrained, informed, and framed by material circumstances" (278). These lives entail the necessity of care. For Wood, care is a hands-on activity, a kind of attitude as well as a kind of work, that demands both time and energy. She describes care as consisting of at least five characteristics: responsiveness to others, sensitivity to others, acceptance of others, patience (the quality of being interruptible), and dynamic autonomy (the ability to hold your own needs as important as the needs of others). That final characteristic is crucial, because it reminds people that care must encompass oneself as well as others. An attitude of care does not require the giving up of self, the denial of one's own knowledge, value, and authority. Instead, it requires a healthy balance of self and other.

Others spinning a fabric of possibilities for caring communication add color and shading to the idea of care consisting of holding authority in creative tension with experience. Sullivan and Goldzwig (1995) suggest a communication method of "relational decision-making," which entails recognition of human interconnectedness and interdependence, the role of symbolic and material contexts, and the humility of persons in power to allow all affected persons to speak and to be heard. Similarly, Foss and Griffin (1995) call for an understanding of communication as suggestion, as evoking possibilities. What they call a "rhetoric of invitation" assumes human equality, the immanent value of all people, and the need for people to determine for themselves what they should and will do. Two modes mark such communication—telling one's own story and allowing others to present theirs in an atmosphere of safety, respect, and equality (7).

Several themes connect these various theories of care in action. *Responsibility* would replace emphasis on individual rights. *Respect* for self and others would structure actions, speech, and relations with one another. *Listening* would be valued as a central communication activity because people would be granted the assumption of a certain level of expertise in their own lives. Communication that seeks *partnership* rather than dominance would serve a common good. Caring communication presents a vision of life where human interdependence, rather than individual autonomy, takes center stage.

COMMUNICATION AND BIRTHING PRACTICES

Care, both in the giving and in the receiving, is a natural response to the human condition. None of us wants to be alone in the world, least of all during times of extreme physical and emotional crisis, such as when we are born, giving birth, or dying. At its most basic level, care means reassurance that we are connected with other humans, that we matter to other people. When we are treated as if we are not connected with other humans, as if we are not even like other humans, we tend to feel controlled rather than cared for.

Four stories drawn from the Birthing Project show distinct situations and pictures of what care looks, sounds, and feels like. The first, that of Lee H., is told by a white woman in her mid-forties during the time of the interview, describing two births that happened in her mid- to late twenties. Controlling communication characterized her experience of the first birth, while caring communication informed the second. Both births took place in a hospital and were managed by doctors. The second story belongs to Elise N., a white woman in her mid-thirties at the time of her interview. Of her three births, the first two ended in cesarean delivery, due to doctors' diagnoses of "failure to progress." Facing the same problem in her third birth, Elise was encouraged by a caring nurse to continue in her efforts toward a vaginal delivery. Elise was successful, and credits the nurse's caring communication for that success. Alexandria O. tells the third story. A forty-six-year-old white woman, Alexandria gave birth vaginally to a breech baby in a hospital, much against the advice of the doctor on call. She had to take care of herself. Her story shows the effort it takes to hold out for self-determination within a communication context that gives the right of decision making to medical personnel. Finally, Dana S. tells the story of a baby born at home before midwives could arrive. She and her husband delivered the baby, she with a sure sense of her own knowledge and power to bring a baby safely into the world virtually by herself. When seen in contrast with the preceding stories, Dana's shows how much influence context exerts over possibilities for caring communication.

LEE H.

Lee's first child had been born twenty-one years prior to her interview, in a hospital that followed normal hospital protocols of the time. Lee's pre-natal care took the shape of what remains a typical medical pattern—monthly short visits with the obstetrician, ending with weekly visits just before the birth. She calls it "typical obstetric care. . . . Cursory, you got your fifteen-minute visits and that was acceptable to me. . . . I assumed this was what care was like" (Lee H. 1996, 1). When labor began, she took the tranquilizer her doctor had prescribed for her. He told her that it would relax her and if her contractions continued after taking the med-ication, she truly was in labor. In hindsight, she rues having taken the pill: "I got talked into having a narcotic on the basis that it would relax me. Again, I felt like, 'I don't need this but I guess they know what they're talking about'" (2). She labored under the influence of the narcotic until she was fully dilated.

Then Lee started pushing to get her baby out. After she had been pushing for an hour, the doctor came in to see her. He told her that the baby seemed big and she seemed small, so it would be a good idea to get a spinal injection. She agreed and says, "I did buy that line. He waited as long as an hour because he knew I wanted a natural childbirth. I'm re-experiencing my anger. At the time, I wasn't angry. At the time, I just felt, 'Oh well. They know what they're doing'" (Lee H. 1996, 3). Her anger is notable because it appeared in hindsight as a response to what she came to see as unwarranted and manipulative communication that controlled her, rather than related to her as a partner.

Lee reports a moment of decision during transition—the period many women talk about as the most intense, exhilarating, and also depressing stage of labor, the period just before the baby moves completely through the birth canal—when she decided to stop pushing because she realized she would be a mother once the baby was out. She says, "After that, I pushed when they told me to but, funny thing, I didn't make any more progress. Of course, at the time, I had no idea that how a woman feels about things has anything to do with labor because I had been told this is a totally mechanical process and I believed it. I didn't say anything about my feelings. Of course, no one would ask me how I was feeling" (Lee H. 1996, 3). Lee's reaction to the situation and to the lack of communication was deep alienation. Further, her ability to give birth was impaired because no one talked with her about what was happening at that point.

After the spinal block, the doctor conducted the birth, cutting Lee open wide and using forceps to pull her baby out. In order to keep Lee from contaminating what the doctor called "the sterile field" (4), Lee's arms were cuffed down by her sides. Control marked virtually every moment of Lee's birthing, even though it was not a risky or even unusually difficult birth.

When Lee's child was born, she couldn't hold him because she was not sterile and her arms were restrained. She says, "I didn't ask for him or protest or anything. I was internalizing all these messages that they were doing things right and the fact that I had a problem with it meant there was something wrong with me" (Lee H. 1996, 5). In this situation, Lee's response to things that would bother her as she thought about them later was to turn against herself. Implicitly, she granted the medical personnel the right to their protocols by saying that she was wrong, she needed to change.

After the birth, the doctor sewed up Lee's episiotomy cut tightly, giving her what she said he called a "love knot" (Lee H. 1996, 8). Later, she found sexual intercourse to be painful. When she discussed it with her doctor, "he said, 'You probably just can't relax. Maybe try a little glass of wine before you make love.' I remember stalking—at this point, I was starting to emerge from that 'there's something wrong with me'—out of his office, thinking, 'What the hell does he know? I've been married seven years. We're not talking about I need to relax a little bit. I'm not a nervous bride" (8). Between the time of birth and this visit, Lee seems to have found a sense of her own value. However, she had not yet reached the point of being able to resist medical control of her by communicating what she knew to be the case.

Lee also had trouble establishing a good breastfeeding relationship with her child. She attributes that to her too-careful attention to the doctor's seemingly expert advice. She says, "There again, I was the compliant patient in that I had been told not to feed the baby any oftener than every three hours, which was total bullshit, but I did it. There again, I was in conflict with my own instincts, walking this crying baby around because it wasn't three hours yet and in tremendous discomfort from the episiotomy" (Lee H. 1996, 6). Here, Lee describes the conflict she felt between her own embodied knowing and what was presented to her as medical knowledge. She gave in to the authority of the medical knowledge, but in hindsight, at the time of this telling, regrets not trusting herself.

Lee's first labor and delivery virtually exemplify the elements and dynamic of controlling communication. She was figured as a patient and a "good girl" who was in pain and needed to be managed in order to get the baby out as efficiently as possible. She felt her knowledge was discounted, and indeed, at the time, she herself discounted her own "instincts," as she calls them. Feeling keenly that she had lost something very important to her quality of life, Lee determined her next birth would be different.

For the second birth, Lee sought out a doctor who she felt listened to her. During prenatal visits, Lee asked what she termed "dumb questions" (Lee H. 1996, 10), feeling confident enough in herself and her doctor to engage in conversation. His responsiveness to her and her concerns encouraged her. During this labor and delivery, Lee asserted herself more than during the first one. The doctor wanted her to take Pitocin, a drug routinely used to increase the intensity of contractions, but she refused, saying she felt her contractions were strong enough. Their earlier relationship, established during prenatal visits, convinced her that he would respect her as a partner during labor and delivery.

Lee's memories of labor were vivid and metaphorical. It seems she experienced this labor more consciously. In describing her state of being, she compares it to being "in a bobsled race where you kind of go whooshing down the hill and the contractions were the curves. . . . Here this powerful thing is happening to your body and you can't say, 'Let's stop for awhile or can I take a break, I'm tired or come back and do this tomorrow'" (Lee H. 1996, 11). In a way, she says, giving birth is like dying, because your body is doing something you can neither control nor stop. She says she felt she was doing something very hard, but this time, "I didn't really doubt my ability to do it if people would just give me the time and space to do it" (14). The comment points up the beneficial qualities of allowing the birth to happen in its own time, a quality of care rather than control. An attitude of control would legitimate intervention authorized by doctors and hospital protocols.

When the time of delivery came, the doctor encouraged her to reach down, pull out her baby, and then hold her. Lee says, "I reached down and he kind of helped me get my hands around the baby and I pulled her up onto my chest. . . . It was like a double image, double exposure, in that instinctively reaching for [my first baby], being restrained by the delivery table cuffs and hearing the doctor say, 'Don't touch. This is a sterile area,' versus birthing my own child, taking that child and pulling that baby up"

(1996, 14). This time, the doctor spoke as a guide, someone encouraging the birthing mother to enter into the learning afforded by the moment. In contrast to the first doctor, this second one shared power with Lee rather than exercising power over her.

Lee frames that birth as a transformational event in her life, where she first saw herself and her body as strong and beautiful because of that strength. She credits the doctor for guiding her to that perception: "It wasn't, 'Thank you doctor for delivering the baby.' It was 'I have given birth,' and that is a powerful distinction that I think women don't get in this culture. They don't think they can do it even if they think it's something important to do, but they're told it's not important to do. And most of them aren't interested because they're told that it's not worth it or even that it's dangerous" (Lee H. 1996, 14). In this statement, Lee indicates her acceptance of the power of birthing, a power her second doctor was willing to share with her.

Both births were hospital births, overseen by doctors. Yet, the stories make it clear that the communication model guiding caregivers dramatically affected the quality of Lee's experience. The first birth was managed according to the model of control, while a care-based model guided the second. When Lee felt as if she were the central participant in the normal life event of a birth, she gained a sense of her own agency and worth, a sense that positively changed how she felt about herself.

ELISE N.

Elise had three births; in the first two, her care followed an escalating trajectory of control based upon medical personnel's perceived need to manage a risky situation. The third birth showed the benefits of shared power between medical personnel and Elise.

Elise's first child was born in a university hospital, complete with all the normal processes and protocols of a hospital in which new doctors are being trained. Elise was seen and examined during her labor by many different doctors and nurses. She says, "Over the course of the eighteen hours that I labored, I bet I had vaginal exams by no fewer than ten different groups of people who were walking around. And I mean groups of people" (Elise N. 1996, 5). Her cervical dilation progressed no further than six centimeters, yet she felt a tremendous need to push out her baby. Her nurse told her not to push, since Elise was not fully dilated. Soon, the doctor decided to deliver her baby by cesarean surgery. Given the numbers of

people involved in her treatment and her own inexperience, Elise was
unable to participate as a partner in her own birthing.

For the birth of her second child, Elise chose a doctor who was a
woman, hoping to find more empathy from her and also support for a
vaginal delivery after cesarean. That did not prove to be the case. Again,
Elise reached six centimeters of dilation and felt a tremendous urge to
push. Her doctor and the nurse told her not to push. According to Elise,
they said, "You can't push. You'll break your scar and you'll rupture the
uterus if you push. You can't push until you're fully dilated" (Elise N.
1996, 14). Shortly after that point, the doctor completed delivery by
cesarean surgery. Elise viewed this second attempt at vaginal birthing as a
kind of failure, one that she bitterly regretted. She resolved to succeed at a
vaginal birth with her next child.

When her third child was due, Elise lived in a different city and had a
different set of doctors and nurses. Her labor progressed much as it had the
first time, with a stopping point at six centimeters of dilation. She says she
felt a lot of support from her nurses, especially one who had to go off duty
at 4:00 P.M. This distressed Elise, but her next nurse met her needs for care.
Elise says, "She was close and physical with me and in a very supportive
way very touching and helped keep me sane in the transition between [the
first and second nurse]" (Elise N. 1996, 24). Soon, Elise reached the six-
centimeter point again and felt the urge to push. At first, the nurse and doctor told her to resist the urge, but when she and her second nurse were
alone, the nurse put her hand inside Elise, on her cervix, and suggested she
push just a little bit. When Elise pushed, her cervix dilated immediately to
eight centimeters.

Elated, Elise waited for the doctor, expecting a go-ahead on a vaginal
delivery. She says, "The doctor came in about 5:10 and he gave me an
internal exam . . . and said, 'She's back down to six again,' and I said, 'Oh,
God,' and the nurse said, 'She is not. Look again doctor. You're determining this based on her vaginal ring, which is not six centimeters. This is ten
centimeters.' And he did another exam a little bit . . . feeling a little bit
more deeply and said, 'Oh, you're right. She is at ten" (Elise N. 1996, 26).
Elise was able to deliver her third baby vaginally, an accomplishment that
gave her great joy. She says, "being actively, physically involved in the
bringing of that child . . . was better than passively receiving my child
through surgery" (37). She credits the success to her nurse and doctor for
their willingness to listen to her and to believe she knew her body well
enough to know when it was time to push.

This is an example of birthing partnership, of caring communication. Even though accepted obstetric protocol strongly suggested a third cesarean delivery, even though Elise would have acquiesced to the surgery if pressed, her nurse, and later, her doctor, gave her the permission she needed to trust herself and to try herself. Her nurse respected Elise by listening and responding in just the way Elise needed her to, by sharing responsibility for the decision. The two of them and her doctor worked together to bring her baby into the world in the way that Elise desired. This was a caring act because it was expressed as such by the medical personnel and experienced as such by Elise. It required the nurse and doctor to release control and to give real choice to Elise. In so doing, they treated her as a full human being who had access to knowledge about her body that their initial observations did not confirm. They trusted her, even when their scientific expertise and observations guided by experience suggested that she was wrong. Sharing both potential risks and rewards, the nurse and doctor and Elise enacted care.

ALEXANDRIA O.

Alexandria O., a forty-six-year-old white woman, had given birth to her baby just three weeks before her interview. While Lee H.'s story contrasts her experience of control and care in two births, and Elise N's features the breakthrough of one caring act of communication, Alexandria's story dramatically shows the obstacles a birthing woman faces when she decides to take care of herself within the context of medical control. As defined earlier in this chapter, care entails a healthy sense of one's own value and the willingness to maintain one's position in balance with the needs and desires of another. In this particular case, Alexandria remained true to her resolve to deliver her breech baby vaginally, even when the attending doctor tried to persuade her that act would put her baby at risk. She did not believe the baby was at risk and took care of herself and her baby as she saw fit, eventually forcing the hospital personnel to meet her terms of care.[1]

Alexandria presents a special case, in any context. For one thing, as a forty-six-year-old, first-time mother, she would be defined as high risk by both doctors and midwives because of her age. In the medical model, any woman over the age of thirty-five is defined as "elderly." Alexandria found a doctor who considered her to be normal, because, as she says, "I had no symptoms of high risk, except for my age" (Alexandria O. 1996,

1). A fit person, Alexandria exercised aerobically throughout her pregnancy. So, physically, although she entered motherhood late in her reproductive life, she considered herself ready for it.

Emotionally, Alexandria had a harder time with her pregnancy. She had been pregnant before, but had lost two at four months and had no success with implantation of two in vitro embryos. So, she says, "I was so afraid of losing this little guy—I tried not to get too attached until the very end, until I knew he could survive if he came premature. And then I started having a relationship with him" (Alexandria O. 1996, 1–2).

When Alexandria began her labor, her doctor was out of town at a conference about a forty-five-minute drive away. There were two doctors on duty at the hospital, one ready to retire and very concerned about malpractice suits and one who was young and untrained in varieties of vaginal deliveries. When Alexandria came to the hospital, her cervix had dilated to six centimeters, so the labor was quite advanced. When she was checked vaginally, the younger doctor found her baby to be in the breech position, meaning the baby's head was up and its bottom was lodged down in the birth canal. Immediately, the doctor told her to get ready for a cesarean delivery. He wanted her to stay in bed, accept an intravenous drip of medication that could be continued during the surgery, and get ready for a cesarean delivery.

Alexandria reports telling him, "'You're not putting an IV in me, because I have not decided to have a c-section. There's nothing wrong with the baby, there's nothing wrong with me. What can be done?'" (Alexandria O. 1996, 7). The doctor continued to press her to consent to a c-section, and she fired him. She said, "'I don't trust you anymore, and I will not allow you to deliver my baby and you can leave this room.' Because, I said, 'You've been badgering me and fighting with me, you're fighting with a woman in second stage labor and you're screaming at her and I don't trust you anymore, and you are not going to be my doctor no matter what, so you can just leave'" (8).

After firing the on-duty doctor, Alexandria and her husband called other hospitals to see if any would accept her at that stage of labor and enable her to deliver vaginally. None would. So Alexandria had the older on-duty doctor call her own doctor at the conference and have her return in order to deliver Alexandria's baby. By the time her doctor arrived, Alexandria had dilated to nine centimeters, just one centimeter removed from full dilation, and was feeling an urge to push. At that point, her doctor encouraged her to have an epidural anesthetic administered. Alexandria resisted, having made it all that way without any anesthetic. However, her doctor persevered, saying she didn't want to use forceps to get the baby out, and would need to get her hands inside Alexandria. The anesthetic would help make that less painful. Alexandria finally consented, and the baby was born whole and healthy.

After the baby was born, Alexandria says the nurses scolded her for breaking hospital policy and jeopardizing her baby. She reports, "That was the attitude—there was an attitude that maybe I had put my baby at risk. Well, the pediatrician came in and said, 'You did the right thing. Your baby was never at risk.' That shut up some of the nurses, but all of them didn't. It was just a rift. It was like the whole place was in an uproar for what I did. All I did was have a semi-natural birth, with a whole lot of interference from them" (Alexandria O. 1996, 11). By not behaving like a patient and cooperating with hospital protocol, Alexandria found herself threatening the entire system, rather than encouraging them to rethink both their treatment of her and cesarean delivery protocols more generally.

In retrospect, Alexandria comments on how she responded to people who asked her why she resisted cesarean delivery so vehemently:

> And I kept saying, "Because I know this is not supposed to be a c-section. I know that everything's okay and he's supposed to come out vaginally. . . . And I have a sense that everything's okay and you're not supposed to operate on me." And that didn't go over real big. But I said it a couple of times, saying that's just a sense I have—that that's the way it's supposed to be. . . . And then I also had this feeling that it wasn't safe for me to have a c-section for some reason. I don't know. My gut was so strong. I've never relied on myself so much. And my husband kept saying, "How do you know?" And I kept saying, "Dear, I don't know how I know. I just know." And he said, "Well, Alexandria, you know what, I trust you and I'm going with you. I'm betting on you." . . . I had no preconceptions on how he was supposed to be delivered. And I was not opposed to a c-section, because I said if anything goes wrong, of course, I'd be more than happy to do a c-section in surgery. I don't know. I just knew. (1996, 12)

Her repetition of "I don't know. I just know" is notable. She experienced a sure sense of the authority of her own knowledge, a sense that sustained her as she resisted the control the hospital personnel tried to exercise over her. She took responsibility for herself. When her own doctor returned to help with the delivery, she included Alexandria in the decision to have an epidural anesthetic administered. She did not coerce Alexandria, but instead offered reasons why it would be a good thing to do. In so doing, her doctor treated Alexandria as a partner in the process of birthing, rather than as a patient who needs to be controlled into accepting what the doctor orders.

It is striking how Alexandria maintained the authority of her knowledge over the doctor's knowledge and her husband's fears. She recalls, "I was never scared at any point throughout this whole thing. I just knew that it was okay, and I had a sense that everything was just fine. My husband's fear . . . was just my husband's fear. He was separate from me. I mean he was there, but I wasn't afraid of anything. I just knew that everything was okay. I still don't know how I knew, but I did" (Alexandria O. 1996, 12).

In contrast to Lee, Alexandria does not represent herself as a "good girl," well socialized to accepting others' definitions of situation, role, and acceptable behavior. Alexandria's story shows an extraordinary sense of self-knowledge and trust, strongly maintained within the symbolic and literal world of the hospital. Her story also shows the amount of work a birthing woman must do to resist the "moving train" of hospital protocols. Once a woman enters the hospital, the entire set of assumptions of staff and institution is that she will submit to the medical model for safety's sake, and, unlike Alexandria and like Lee during her first birth and Elise during her three births, most women in labor find themselves submitting rather than resisting. Resisting during the trying physical and emotional exertions of labor calls for an extraordinary summoning of will.

DANA S.

This chapter's final story tells about a home birth, one where midwifery ideals rather than hospital protocols structured the situation. Dana, a white woman, twenty-nine years old at the time of the interview, has had two homebirths. When she was pregnant with her first child, she saw a doctor at first. During an early visit, he made a joke about finding out her husband's penis size so the doctor would know how tightly he would need to sew Dana up after the birth. He also informed her that she would most likely have to have an episiotomy, because in his experience, "99 percent of first moms need" them (Dana S. 1996, 2). Further, during a hospital tour, her husband was told that if he became argumentative about some procedure deemed medically necessary during her labor and delivery, he would be removed by security. So, rather than remain in a situation where they felt they would be forced to fit predetermined norms, Dana and her husband decided to seek out certified nurse midwives to guide them through a home birth. Fortunately, their insurance at the time covered such a process.

During the course of labor in her first birth, Dana dilated quickly to ten centimeters, but then felt no urge to push her baby out. Unbeknownst to her, the midwives were required by the laws of the state to take her to a hospital after two hours of "unproductive" pushing. Dana says, "If I'd known that, I might have declined the examination. . . . What's going on in my mind is, 'It doesn't hurt yet, so I'm in early labor. It's going to hurt and I'm going to be able to handle it, but it's going to hurt. I need to conserve my strength until it starts hurting'" (Dana S. 1996, 4). As the clock ticked, the midwives urged her to push, even though she did not feel like it yet. So she did, but she tore and she got hemorrhoids. Even though the baby was born safely at home, Dana felt manipulated by her midwives' fear.

Not satisfied with the birth she felt the certified nurse midwives had conducted through a medical model, complete with its legally based protocols, Dana sought out lay midwives for her second birth. She and her family had moved after the first birth. New to the state, she joined a group of women interested in alternative birthing practices and started asking around for references for lay midwives. She was met with a resounding silence. Unbeknownst to her, shortly before this time, a lay midwife had been arrested and sued for practice without a license. Finally, Dana met up with a woman who had just "caught one baby by accident" (Dana S. 1996, 11) and asked her to serve as midwife.

As the pregnancy progressed, the women in the group grew to trust Dana, and she offered to act as a "guinea pig" (Dana S. 1996, 11) for lay midwives in training. Although they were outside the law, and also outside control by the American Medical Association, this set of midwives were training each other. A requirement of training was to observe home births and to "catch" a certain number of babies.[2]

Shortly after the thirty-sixth week of pregnancy, Dana went into labor at about 3:30 one morning. She and her husband called a number of people to attend and watch the birth. While her husband was on the phone and then looking around the kitchen for a big bowl, Dana made her slow way toward the bathroom and took a rest on a futon on the floor. She says, "I never did get up from that futon" (Dana S. 1996, 16).

Dana called her husband up to the futon after a contraction and told him to stay with her. She says, "I had this intellectual realization that I was holding back. I realized, 'I'm holding back.' So, I decided that during the next contraction, I was just going to open up and see what happened. During that contraction, I felt a kind of popping which it wasn't the water breaking but I remember my mother saying when my sister was born that she felt a pop and that was when she went to her room to lie down. It wasn't her water breaking. Her water had already broken. I felt that pop" (Dana S. 1996, 16). This characterization of the relative role of mind and body differs significantly from that expressed by women in the Birthing Project who chose medical treatment during labor and delivery. Women who choose hospitals and doctors tend to let the doctors' observations and the monitoring machines' output become the symbolic reality of the birth. In Dana's words, we can see a high degree of consciousness about the ways in which her mind and body were related.

With her husband in attendance, Dana moved quickly toward birth. She says, I "remember what happened during each contraction. I was really aware of it. I was really aware of the baby moving. The baby would move a lot during each contraction. When I was pushing, I wasn't trying to push. I was lying on my left side and I think my husband was holding my right leg up a little because I asked him to. I wasn't pushing on purpose but during a contraction, everything would just tense up and then, after a few seconds, it would relax. It was while I relaxed that the baby moved. Not while it was tense" (Dana S. 1996, 17). As Dana tells it, her body worked in concert with the baby. Her attitude was one of attention and interest in what she experienced as a unity of effort between herself and the baby.

Soon, Dana's water broke and gushed all over her husband. He was astonished. According to Dana, "He said, 'You never told me the baby was coming.' 'I'm in labor, what does that mean to you?' He said, 'It took several hours the first time.' He figured he had time to go look for a bowl for me to throw up in. . . . Poor man!" (Dana S. 1996, 17). Meanwhile, "when the water broke," Dana says, "I felt a huge movement and I could tell during the next contraction that the baby's head was in the vagina. The baby had gone through . . ." (17). Realizing the baby would be born before any of the midwives or midwives in training could arrive, Dana directed her husband to get a syringe ready to squeeze fluid out of the baby's nose. She told him to put his hands around the baby's head and to press on Dana's skin so the head and shoulders would not tear her. Her husband pulled the baby out when she told him to. Relaxing, she lay there with her baby on her belly while her husband used towels to clean up. The midwives arrived in time to help deliver the placenta.

When asked what advice she would give women planning to have babies, Dana emphatically encouraged mothers-to-be to seek caregivers who would be positive about the mothers' ability to deliver their babies:

> If anybody says anything to you that makes it sound like they don't think that you are going to be able to have your baby: "I'm worried because your baby is too big"; "I'm worried because your pelvis is too small"; "I'm worried because this baby is too late"—if somebody specifically says to you, "I don't think that you can give birth to this baby"—that's a problem. If your doctor or your midwife thinks you can't give birth to your baby, you need to go find another one, even if you are forty-one weeks. You need to find somebody who actually believes you are going to have your baby because people who think you are going to have your baby will stand there and watch you have your baby. People who don't think you can have your baby will help you out. (Dana S. 1996, 21)

Clearly, from Dana's point of view, it is far better to have your baby on your own terms than to have someone help you have your baby on their terms.

Dana's confidence in her ability to bring a baby into the world is unique among the women I interviewed, in that, essentially, she took care of herself and the birth, with minimal help from her husband, confident in her ability to handle the situation. Not a single woman who chose an obstetrician and hospital represented herself as so confident. Even among the women who chose midwives and home births, Dana's level of assurance in herself and her baby was rarely matched. In her case, this was just what she wanted. She gave and received the care she believed she needed and was satisfied with its outcome.

WHO KNOWS?

Medical practice presents an interesting case for discussing the pragmatic effects on human life of care- or control-based communication. In the United States, birthing has come to be defined as a medical event, tinged with risk, which warrants control by expert medical personnel, particularly doctors. In contrast, in the Netherlands, as well as other countries, birthing is perceived to be a natural event, not often attended by risk (Katz Rothman [1982] 1991; Jordan 1983). These two points of view may be termed the "medical model," in which the need to control the "patient" in the name of her good and the good of the child is paramount, and the midwifery model, in which the need to care for a mother in the name of her own good takes priority. One need not be a doctor in order to adhere to the medical model, nor (as was seen in the case of Lee's second doctor) be a midwife to subscribe to the midwifery model. The models refer instead to preferred systems of communicating.

Within the medical model, the point of view, as well as the authority, of the observer is privileged. In a landmark work on American ways of birthing, Barbara Katz Rothman ([1982] 1991) notes, "The foremost 'beholder' of pregnancy in America today is the obstetrician. The obstetrical perspective on pregnancy and birth is held to be not just one way of looking at it, but to be the truth" (33). The "truth" of the medical model is that an observer (in this case, a doctor) is seen as better capable of making objective, scientific judgments based on knowledge of a large number of cases. Observers know what can and might happen because their knowledge has been obtained through training (reading and watching other expert observers) and personal observation.

While the major characters in the story of control told within the medical model are the medical personnel, and the obstetrician in particular, the presenting situation is the potentially risky act of delivering a baby from a woman's body, so the only place birth should occur is where it is most able to be controlled—at a hospital. As the one who knows, the doctor takes responsibility for making decisions and the woman plays the role of patient. What counts as unacceptable or acceptable practices follows upon the heels of the ideology: unacceptable practices are those that deviate from normal protocol (rules for expected responses to typical situations), and acceptable practices follow protocol. Within the medical model, justification for action depends upon medically warranted principles that put the good of the baby at the center. In the medical model, the woman is a necessary means to the end of a healthy baby's birth, but she is more an object to be controlled and managed through reducing her pain, mobility, and decision making than a subject to be respected as a knowing partner.

In contrast, the midwifery model positions women as knowledgeable subjects, well able to know their own bodies, their children within them, and the best way to give birth. Instead of the baby being the focus of attention, a "good birth" is seen as the appropriate end. If the birth is good, the baby and mother both will be well. The role of the midwife is to care for the woman in such a way that she herself gives birth to the baby, while the role of the woman is to take responsibility for herself and her child. The situation is defined as natural, normal, and family-based. As such, it may take place wherever a woman is most comfortable, not just in a hospital but perhaps at home or in a birthing center. As before, acceptable and unacceptable practices follow from the ideology. Acceptable practices are those deemed so by the laboring woman; unacceptable, the same. The woman and her baby are seen as a pair, a couple, not as a conflicting dyad. As Katz Rothman ([1982] 1991) suggests, "In the midwifery model, mother and fetus genuinely are one, and that which meets the needs of the one meets the needs of the other" (48). The job of the midwife is to enable a woman to trust her own knowledge on how to give birth, not to deliver the baby.

In graphic terms, here are the elements of the medical model and the midwifery model:

MEDICAL MODEL	MIDWIFERY MODEL
1. Observational knowledge is privileged.	1. Experiential knowledge is privileged.
2. Doctors control the experience.	2. Mothers control the experience.
3. Babies' needs and safety take precedence.	3. Mothers' and babies' needs are considered together.
4. Protocol takes precedence over individual differences.	4. Individual differences take precedence over protocol.
5. Mothers are patients who are in pain.	5. Mothers are subjects who are engaged in the productive work of birthing.
6. Pregnancy and birth are abnormal.	6. Pregnancy and birth are normal.

In the United States, the hegemony of the medical model in setting what counts as knowledge has been well documented (Ehrenreich and English 1973, 1989; Jordan 1983; Katz Rothman [1982] 1991; Mitford 1992; Nelson 1996; Oakley 1980, 1984; Sterk 1996). Further, popular culture represents only the medical model as a safe option for birthing women (Sterk 1996). Therefore, not only do past and current birthing practices presume the medical model, so too do the sources of knowledge available to laypersons, particularly women making choices about their birth care.

The kind of possibilities for control contained within cultural expectations for birth are compounded by the roles women are presumed to play, particularly within the hospital setting. First, if they give birth in hospitals,

they are positioned as "patients." Talcott Parsons's 1951 schema of role
expectations for patients still has explanatory power. He says patients are
expected by the medical institution to fulfill four roles:

1. Exemption from normal social responsibilities
2. Exemption from responsibility for the sickness
3. Motivation to get well as soon as possible
4. Cooperation in seeking technically competent help (436–37)

Patients are assumed to be incompetent and need to be either cajoled
or coerced into passive acceptance of medical expertise. If patients choose
not to accept the role, they are framed as obstreperous, as irrational, as
not being concerned for their own and others' safety.

Add to this role the normal gender expectations of women within a
patriarchal culture. Of all writers on gender, Sandra Bem (1993) best names
the three key characteristics of gender construction within patriarchy:

1. *Gender polarization*—meaning the assumption that women and
   men are distinctly different, even opposite of one another.
2. *Androcentrism*—meaning that men are the measure of humanity.
   Whatever is not-male is less-than-human.
3. *Biological essentialism*—meaning that women and men just are
   what they are by virtue of their biology, not by virtue of symbolic
   constructions of meaning. (2–3)

When women give birth in hospitals, not only are they patients, with
the attendant expectations of docility in the face of medical expertise, but
they are women, as well, subject to male authority while they are in the
throes of what medicine defines as a purely physical act, whose positive
outcome is defined as a healthy baby, not necessarily a good birth.

It should be recognized that this particular patient role is hemmed all
about by expectations set by gender and masculine hegemony. All birthing
women are women, and the American medical institution has been constructed according to male norms and standards. Women may be doctor
and nurse, but the institution itself is imprinted with male perspectives
(Albers and Savitz 1991; Ehrenreich and English 1973, 1989; Hagell 1989;
McCool and McCool 1989; Mitford 1992; Vosler and Burst 1993). A person who is doing what may be seen as the paradigmatically female act,
giving birth, within a context that labels her a patient, faces severe limits

on her agency to assert herself as a knowing agent, responsible for her own actions. Not only do the medical institution and medical personnel tell her what to do and subject her to set protocols, she herself has internalized both patient and gender expectations, and so will connive in her own pacification. Only a rare person is aware enough of her own embodied knowing to maintain her will against the institution's authority. Within a communication system predicated on control such as this, both women and medical personnel lose. Women lose their sense of authority and self-worth, and medical personnel lose the valuable insights they might gain from listening to women explaining their own experiences.

HOW MIGHT AN ETHIC OF CARE GUIDE DECISION MAKING?

A caring orientation toward others also carries its own pitfalls for participants, namely paternalism/maternalism (where the caregivers' sense of superior expertise leads them to ignore the cared-for-person's point of view) and parochialism (seeing current, local concerns as the only true reality) (Tronto 1993). Tronto maintains that the solution to these two pitfalls is "to insist that care needs to be connected to a theory of justice and to be relentlessly democratic in its disposition" (170). This caveat warns participants to attend both to individual rights and to interpersonal responsibilities.

In the case of birthing care, I would suggest that this idea frames the birthing woman as actively engaged in an ultimately healthy endeavor, instead of passively undergoing a medical procedure. Further, it suggests all birthing women be treated this way, not just privileged ones. So, at the least, an ethic of care would require birth caregivers listen to women and take the women's opinions and preferences into consideration when deliberating.

Five guidelines of a care-based ethical consciousness can guide caring communication, particularly in the context of birthing. These guidelines have been adapted from Lerner's (1993) scheme of the constituent parts of feminist consciousness.

First, people need to be aware that they are located within a symbolically maintained system of power relations.

This awareness needs to be held both by caregivers and cared-for people. Doctors, nurses, and midwives who work in hospitals operate within a hierarchically structured medical institution. McCool and McCool's (1989) historical overview of nurse-midwifery points out that the profession of midwifery has been and remains suppressed by the American Medical Association, and in general, that doctors have controlled the ways in which medicine will be practiced in America. Vosler and Burst (1993) detail the constraints that doctors have placed on the relation between midwives and birthing women in hospitals. The system of birthing in American hospitals is marked by an attitude of control, protocol, and order. In this context, giving care to birthing women is neither simple nor straightforward. As can be seen in the case of the second nurse in Elise's story, by offering real care, one runs the risk of violating hospital protocol, a risk that could cost a nurse a job, a midwife her hospital privileges. So, some strategic awareness, on the part of both caregivers and people cared for, of the limits as well as the possibilities of a given care situation is crucial.

Second, people need to realize that they have some level of power within that system.

No matter how little power it may be, everyone—caregivers and cared-for people—holds some power within the system. Even though hospitals may be run as medical institutions, complete with rules, protocols, and practices, birthing women have the power to refuse treatment, to expect answers to questions, and to be allowed some latitude of choice. If they are not given that power, and do not choose to exercise it, as was the case with Lee during her first birthing experience, women may well feel impotence and anger. Caregivers may exercise discretion in following rules. When and if they do, as did the nurse and the doctor in Elise's third birth, they share power with birthing women. Sharing power increases people's sense of their own value, and ultimately, their own humanity.

Third, people need to see others as engaged with them.

A care-based perspective on how relations should be constructed between medical personnel and birthing women would be founded on a belief in human interdependence. Researchers, especially feminists, who push against the modernist assumptions of autonomous individuality as the paradigm of humanity are moving understanding toward the concept that humans are most fully human in relation with one another (Foss and

Griffin 1992, 1995; Keller 1986; Noddings 1984; Sterk and Turner 1994; Tronto 1993; and Wood 1994, among others). Therefore, actions and communication that cut off connection between people are perceived as less caring than those that maintain a sense of mutuality.

> *Fourth, people need to be encouraged to tell the stories*
> *of their own situations.*

This guideline stresses the phenomenological basis of care. As Nel Noddings so well articulates it, care counts as care only if the receiver sees it as such. So, the only way to know how well one is caring is to listen to the stories of the cared-for people. Nursing researchers Kennedy (1995) and Hagell (1989) explicitly endorse such a perspective, calling upon nurses to come to know the people they care for through their stories, respecting the people enough not to discount their experiences as naive.

All too few resources presenting women's stories of their own acts of giving birth exist. A recent review of popularly available birthing literature turned up very few books containing a wide range of women's first-person stories, told in their own voices (Sterk 1996). Even at best, most such books filter women's stories through the perspective of the expert, as does Dwinell (1992) in her collection, *Birth Stories: Mystery, Power, and Creation.* Dwinell tells women's birthing stories from her perspective as a nurse. Although this certainly is better than not presenting women's stories at all, it still smacks of a paternalistic/maternalistic assumption that stories told by the women themselves are not as trustworthy as those controlled by one with observational, expert knowledge.[3] When women themselves speak, they add direct testimony of internal states and of reception of care that is not accessible to an observer.

> *Fifth, people need to develop a vision of mutual care and responsibility.*

This final guideline places demands upon both caregivers and cared-for people. Caregivers need to see themselves as responsible to the people for whom they care. Such responsibility would obligate them to influence through consultative dialogue rather than to control through directive, one-way talk. Lee's second birth story shows how that would occur. She saw her doctor as a partner, as a guide, rather than as an authority. That doctor explained what he was doing during labor and guided Lee through her experience, working with her rather than over her.

Cared-for people, as well, need to see themselves as responsible for the quality of their care. Birthing women need to inform themselves well about their own condition and about varieties of treatments that might be performed, and they must formulate their agreement or disagreement to those treatments. In order to be a partner with their caregiver, they must bring knowledge and informed opinion to the birthing situation. This requires women to play an active role, such as the one played by Alexandria, not a passive role. They need to read, ask questions, listen to other women's stories, prepare a birthing plan, and require the hospital personnel or other caregiver to consider both it and the woman's ongoing needs carefully.

This final guideline may be the most difficult to implement, yet it is the most crucial. It is difficult to implement because it goes against the grain of the way the particular symbolic institution of hospitals is constructed. Cared-for people are positioned as patients, with the entailment of passive response to procedures and protocols. Furthermore, just as people are indoctrinated to accept hospital care, caregivers are conditioned to work within their system, not to adjust it to the needs of each individual cared-for person.

Dealing honestly with this last guideline may lead birthing women to choose a birthing context, such as a birthing center or a home birth, that allows them to exercise partnerships with their caregivers, as did Dana. Indeed, it may lead (and has led) caregivers to leave the controlling context of traditional medical institutions and to set up independent care centers or offer home birthing services.

In summary, it may be seen that caregivers, especially when working with birthing women (who are going through a natural, not a medical event), will exercise better care by giving a reasonable measure of control to the women themselves. Care is not care when it controls, unless an emergency occurs. In such a case, of course, responsible caregivers will use their best judgment to avert catastrophe. However, the vast majority of births are "uneventful," at least as far as emergencies go. So, generally speaking, in birthing situations, control counts as care when it is control released by the caregiver to the cared-for person. Birthing women's care is best served when caregivers' communication educates and influences through presenting possibilities and options. This education needs to begin well before labor and should be carried through to the end of delivery.

Mary Belenkey and her colleagues, in *Women's Ways of Knowing* (1986), use the metaphor of midwifery to explain how women should be taught. They present a midwife as encouraging a woman to understand her body and her developing fetus, to know about the process of birthing, and to give her the power to deliver her child. In midwife-directed birth, they say, the delivery belongs to the woman. *She* brings forth the child.

This is a great metaphor, yet I would suggest one does not need to be a midwife in order to think and act in this way. In both Lee's and Elise's cases, medical personnel treated them as knowing partners in the delivery of their children. Good caregiving grows out of an attitude of adaptability and possibility. It encourages choice by the birthing women and is conducted by the means of listening and appropriate response. Good caregiving aims at partnership, rather than power.

NOTES

1. In the current medical climate, driven by fear of malpractice suits, in which doctors are held liable if they do not follow protocols that rely on available technology, the assumption is that breech births cannot be managed safely through vaginal birth. Indeed, some obstetric programs do not even teach students how to deliver a breech baby vaginally, instead recommending cesarean delivery. However, a thorough review of the medical literature on the safety of vaginal versus cesarean deliveries of babies in breech positions has shown no significant difference in outcomes, either for mothers or for babies, between the two (Goer 1995).

2. The American system of birth does not make it easy for a woman to seek and secure midwife care for home births. In Dana's case, since she was living in a different state and her husband's insurance differed from that during her first birth, the expense of Dana's second home birth was not covered. During her second pregnancy, Dana also saw a doctor, so that if she had to go to the hospital for an emergency during the birth, her pregnancy would be certified by her HMO and her care covered. After the baby was born, the HMO paid her doctor the entire fee he would have been paid if he had delivered the baby—$3,500. In addition, Dana paid the midwives $2,000 of her own money.

3. For a taste of women's own stories, I recommend Sterk and Sterk's (1993) chapter, "Birthing: Women Owning Their Stories"; Leona VandeVusse's (1993) dissertation, "Personal Meanings of Control Reported by Women in Their Birth Stories: A Feminist Perspective"; and the Birthing Project archive collection of women's stories held at Marquette University.

REFERENCES

Albers, L. L., and D. A. Savitz. 1991. Hospital setting for birth and use of medical procedures in low-risk women. *Journal of Nurse-Midwifery* 36:327–33.

Alexandria O. 1996. Interview by Helen Sterk, 28 May. Available at Memorial Library Archives, Marquette University, Milwaukee, WI 53201.

Bem, S. 1993. *The lenses of gender.* New Haven, Conn.: Yale University Press.

Belenkey M. F., B. M. Clinchy, N. R. Goldberger, and J. M. Tarule. 1986. *Women's ways of knowing: The development of self, voice, and mind.* New York: Basic Books.

Blair, C., J. R. Brown, and L. A. Baxter. 1994. Disciplining the feminine. *Quarterly Journal of Speech* 80:383–409.

Dana S. 1996. Interview by Helen Sterk, 9 May. Available at Memorial Library Archives, Marquette University, Milwaukee, WI 53201.

Dwinell, J. 1992. *Birth stories: Mystery, power and creation.* Westport, Conn.: Bergin and Garvey.

Ehrenreich, B., and D. English. 1973. *Witches, midwives, and nurses: A history of women healers.* Old Westbury, N.Y.: Feminist Press.

———. 1989. *For her own good: One hundred and fifty years of experts' advice to women.* New York: Doubleday.

Elise N. 1996. Interview by Helen Sterk, n.d. Available at Memorial Library Archives, Marquette University, Milwaukee, WI 53201.

Foss, S. K., and C. L. Griffin. 1992. A feminist perspective on rhetorical theory: Toward a clarification of boundaries. *Western Journal of Communication* 56:330–49.

———. 1995. Beyond persuasion: A proposal for invitational rhetoric. *Communication Monographs* 62:2–18.

Goer, H. 1995. *Obstetric myths versus research realities: A guide to medical literature.* Westport, Conn.: Bergin and Garvey.

Griffin, C. 1996. The essentialist roots of the public sphere: A feminist critique. *Western Journal of Communication* 60:21–39.

Hagell, E. I. 1989. Nursing knowledge: Women's knowledge. A sociological perspective. *Journal of Advanced Nursing* 14:226–33.

Jordan, B. 1983. *Birth in four cultures: A cross-cultural investigation of childbirth in Yucatan, Holland, Sweden, and the United States.* Montreal: Eden Press.

Katz Rothman, B. [1982]. 1991. *In labor: Women and power in the birthplace.* New York: W.W. Norton.

Keller, C. 1986. *From a broken web: Separation, sexism and self.* Boston: Beacon Press.

Kennedy, H. P. 1995. The essence of nurse-midwifery care: The woman's story. *Journal of Nurse-Midwifery* 40:410–17.

Lee H. 1996. Interview by Helen Sterk, 23 May. Available from Memorial Library Archives, Marquette University, Milwaukee, WI 53201.

Lerner, G. 1993. *The creation of feminist consciousness: From the middle ages to 1880*. New York: Oxford University.

McCool, W., and S. J. McCool. 1989. Feminism and nurse-midwifery: Historical overview and current issues. *Journal of Nurse-Midwifery* 34:323–34.

Mimi W. 1996. Interview by Helen Sterk, 4 April. Available from Memorial Library Archives, Marquette University, Milwaukee, WI 53201.

Mitford, J. 1992. *The American way of birth*. New York: Penguin.

Nelson, E. 1996. The American experience of childbirth: Toward a range of safe choices. In *Evaluating women's health messages: A resource book*, ed. R. L. Parrott and C. M. Condit, 106–23. Thousand Oaks, Calif.: Sage Publications.

Noddings, N. 1984. *Caring: A feminine approach to ethics and moral education*. Berkeley: University of California Press.

Oakley, Ann. 1980. *Women confined: Toward a sociology of childbirth*. New York: Schocken Books.

———. 1984. *The captured womb: A history of the medical care of pregnant women*. Oxford: Basil Blackwell.

Parsons, T. 1951. *The social system*. Glencoe, Ill.: Free Press.

Ruddick, S. 1989. *Maternal thinking: Toward a politics of peace*. New York: Ballantine Books.

Sterk, H. 1996. Contemporary Birthing Practices: Technology over humanity? In *Evaluating women's health messages: A resource book*, ed. R. L. Parrott and C. M. Condit, 124–34. Thousand Oaks, Calif.: Sage Publications.

Sterk, H., and K. Sterk. 1993. Birthing: Women owning their stories. In *Communication and sex-role socialization*, ed. C. Berryman-Fink, D. Ballard-Reisch, and L. H. Newman, 433–61. New York: Garland Press.

Sterk, H., and L. Turner. 1994. Gender, communication, and community. In *Differences that make a difference: Examining the assumptions in gender research*, ed. L. Turner and H. Sterk, 213–21 Westport, Conn.: Bergin & Garvey.

Sullivan, P. A., and S. R. Goldzwig. 1995. A relational approach to moral decision-making: The majority opinion in Planned Parenthood v. Casey. *Quarterly Journal of Speech* 81:167–90.

Tronto, J. 1993. *Moral Boundaries: A political argument for an ethic of care*. New York: Routledge.

VandeVusse, L.G. 1993. Personal meanings of control reported by women in their birth stories: A feminist perspective. Ph.D. diss., University of Wisconsin-Milwaukee.

Vosler, A. T., and H. V. Burst. 1993. Nurse-midwifery as it reinforces and transforms the American ideology of gendered roles. *Journal of Nurse-Midwifery* 38:293–300.

Wood, J. 1992. Gender and moral voice: Moving from women's nature to standpoint epistemology. *Women's Studies in Communication* 15:1–24.

———. 1994. *Who cares? Women, care and culture.* Carbondale, Ill.: Southern Illinois University Press.

4

BIRTHING ON THE RESERVATION
An Anthropological Perspective

Alice Beck Kehoe

n 1939, a young woman learning anthropology field-work from Ruth Benedict took down memoirs from a respected matron on the Blackfeet Indian Reservation, Montana. These paragraphs are Insima's account of childbirth, translated by her daughter Agnes:[1]

When Agnes had her baby, [her mother] Insima was nearby but not present. Every time Agnes suffered she [Insima] had to run out and cry. Thus she was constantly running in and out. However, she was present at the second birth. (It is always like this—hate to be present at first birth their daughter has. Mother might stay if she felt others are not helping enough and she can do more for her daughter, everyone thinks she is very brave in such a case.)

There was no medicine smoke [healing ritual] at that time. It had been stopped by the [blank; agent or priest?]. If the girl suffers for two or three days, they make a [blank] to bring child right away. Medicine man and wife called on Agnes to change clothes and make medicine so that she does not have another child soon. His wife took care of changing her clothes, and he painted her face yellow.

Gave her no medicine or anything to wear. Told her that if she let no one wear her shawl she would not have another baby right away. He lied, for she had one three years later, and she so informed him. He was paid with a work horse.

When Agnes was five months old [Insima] saw she didn't get enough milk. Asked Mother about it. Mother said, Do you feel different? No, I haven't even menstruated. Then four months later she felt something moving in her stomach. Went and told her Mother. Maybe you're right and I'm pregnant again—I didn't even menstruate again.

Next fall she had a boy. Women told her that the children were so close together maybe they were twins. Boy dies when nine days old.

The priests were there already [a Catholic mission was established in 1881 and the early reservation agents were Methodist ministers (Harrod 1971, 55, 69)]. They took and buried it. She thinks it was the first grave at the mission.

Usually don't have intercourse with husband a month or six weeks after that. Afraid of husband then—don't want to have another child right away but they usually do have a child every two years.

After tenth day, going to get out of bed they put entirely new clothes on. Mother gets any old lady [and tells her] that her girl is getting out of bed and to go help her put them on. When old lady gets there takes all the clothes off. Makes sweet smoke—blankets, moccasins, stockings, etc. and holds them over smoke and then puts the clothes on her. Paints girl's face. Not paid for this. This lady must be old enough to no longer have children. Takes all the girl's old clothes that she wore in bed [including] blanket and she keeps these. This is to keep the girl from being caught right away.

Agnes' 'daughter' [presumably, her cousin (*nitána*) Fine Shield Woman] was married to Mr. [James Willard] Schultz. Almost died when she gave birth to Hart Schultz. P[otato] [Fine Shield Woman's mother] went to Mother and asked her to help her daughter so she wouldn't have any more children. We almost lost her. Father agreed that something should be done.

There was a round copper bracelet with a hole—put a buckskin string through it and put it on the woman's neck. Told her, if a dog has puppies don't pick up or take one—it's all right if they're older and running around—or you'll be caught then. Never did have another child.

This is, so far as I have found, the only direct account of childbirth from a Pikuni[2] woman born before the establishment of the reservations. Insima herself practiced as a midwife and herb doctor, but Benedict's student did not record her knowledge in these fields, noting only that in 1939, at the age of seventy, Insima took advantage of an unplanned stop during a drive on the reservation to run nimbly about the surrounding hills, gathering medicinal plants. In 1996, Ginny F. recalled that when her grandmother, Mrs. Boy Chief, died, Insima had cared for the little girl who would become Ginny F's mother: "Insima was a nice old lady, she helped everybody out. Got a book with her picture in it [*Look at America*, by editors of *Look Magazine*, Houghton Mifflin 1946, 235]. She was really a nice old lady. She raised lots of stepchildren. She did everything, she had all kinds of Indian roots and barks, for diarrhea and so on" (4). Ginny F.'s mother attended Holy Family Mission school on the reservation and then the government boarding school for Indians at Fort Shaw, south of the reservation. She returned to her people to marry, about 1912, and bore three children, bleeding to death in childbirth with the last: as was customary at that time, she awaited the birth at her parents' settlement and was attended only by her sisters, both younger and inexperienced.

Beverly Hungry Wolf, a contemporary member of the Alberta Blackfoot group, the Blood, set down reminiscences of her own childhood with those of her elder female relatives. Her account corroborates and amplifies that of Insima, and Hungry Wolf (1982) adds: "I still often hear of the stereotyped Indian mother who has her child alone, out in some field, and then comes back home and continues her work as if nothing happened. If there were Indians who did this, they were sure not my grandmothers" (190). She describes Blackfoot women's reluctance to instruct girls in the physiology of sex and childbirth until they were married. (Girls' first marriages were customarily arranged by parents soon after menarche, when the girl was about fifteen.) Hungry Wolf emphasizes that "as soon as my grandmothers of the past knew that they were pregnant, they slowed down their work" (190), and their husbands arranged for a younger sister or widowed relative to move in and assist with housework. After the birth, women would continue to take it easy for thirty days, usually in their mothers' homes rather than with their husbands.

Hungry Wolf (1982) published this account of childbirth as told by her grandmother Anada-aki, born in the 1880s:

> When I first thought I was pregnant I just looked at the moon, and I started counting from there. I counted nine moons, and on the tenth moon I went into labor. Some women have a real hard time, and others find it easy. Myself, I went into labor at night. I kept on with it all the next day, that night, and on through the morning. It must have been near noon when my baby was born. We just had our Indian doctor around, and they made brews for us. One of these doctors was called that final morning. My husband gave him his pick of the horses, for payment. When he had picked out his horse he came right in and prayed for me and doctored me. After that I started to feel good and cheerful.
>
> Right after the baby was born and taken care of, my mother started to clean me. After I was cleaned she started massaging my bones back into

place. I was given some broth to drink and then she laid me down to rest. That first baby died because in the excitement my mother cut the navel cord too short and air got into the baby's stomach and killed it. If I had been in a hospital they might have operated and saved it. There was no Indian doctor right there to help. (191–92)

Expectation that sisters will attend each other's birth labors persists among the Pikuni. An interviewee in her early thirties said:

I helped two of my sisters have their babies, I was going to "make like a midwife" or whatever you'd like to call it. The first was to the baby of the family, she's really a small girl and she just had no problem, I stimulated her by talking to her and keeping her on the situation and I'd massage her because she was very tired, you know, didn't really know what to expect, and she was pretty scared. I just talked to her all through and helped her to breathe and showed her how to breathe and she had the baby just fine. And the next one was having her third child but her kids were like, I think, thirteen years apart and her first, she just totally lost it, I really wasn't there to help her at all but the last one was just born a year ago this December, he turned one, and she asked me to help her. I didn't want to but I said OK, so I did and then also I did like to her, just talked to her and I went and got her the root that she needed, this "fishback bone" to, you know, to help the contractions. She was going to, say, take it, she took some and she threw it up, same way, took some more, and then she held it down and she had the baby naturally, with no complications, and that was her best delivery she's ever had. So I mean, it was just keeping her in the moment, talking to her and massaging her that kept her stimulated, you know, and into the moment until what was happening. She had a very healthy baby.

Those of my sisters that I assisted, both of their babies were born in the Browning hospital, in 1987 and 1995 they were born. I've been asked to assist several others but I just haven't really gotten into it. (Laura R. 1996, 2)

Commentary. A common theme in these reminiscences is the community concern with the parturient woman. Her female relatives surround her, her husband summons a midwife or, later, a nurse if one can be brought, and if the labor is protracted, he would have called in a man or woman trained to invoke spiritual power as well as knowledgeable about herbal remedies. The contemporary woman interviewed, quoted above, is a member of an extended family that for several generations has taught and exemplified the Pikuni way of life.

HEALTH SERVICES ON THE RESERVATION

Treaties between the United States and Indian nations generally stipulated that "a medicine chest" should be made available to the Indians. After the final conquests of the First Nations and the establishment of reservations in the 1870s, physicians and nurses were employed by the Bureau of Indian Affairs (B.I.A.) to attend medical needs on the reservations and in the boarding schools promoted to "civilize" Indian children. B.I.A. salaries for medical personnel and funds for hospitals were always lower than national rates, and especially considering that service in remote reservation agency villages could be construed as hardship for a highly educated urban Euro-American, medical staff and facilities available to Indians were, as a rule, poor. With native economies shattered and Indians' development of farming and ranching frequently undermined by inept or corrupt B.I.A. agents, malnutrition increased vulnerability to tuberculosis and other diseases. The limited funds enacted for Indian health targeted the management of tuberculosis and trachoma (Prucha 1986, 290–91). Not until after World War I were hospitals considered appropriate for normal childbirth; the Blackfeet Reservation seems not to have lagged, perhaps because the great distances between settlements induced many women to await birth during the ninth month in town or at an extended family allotment to ensure assistance during labor.

Ginny F., ninety-two years old in 1996, recalled:

My mother [stepmother, married after Ginny's biological mother's death in childbirth] had her babies at home and she had, let's see, she had twelve. The last one she had was a little boy. It was in February and it was a cold winter day and they couldn't get to the hospital, some forty miles or so. My dad went after a nurse about ten miles away. Well, they didn't make it back. They had a lot of trouble in the blizzard and all that cold weather, him and my uncle, to bring the nurse over. The nurse couldn't come. So when she had her baby, she just told me what to do. She told me to go down and warm water up and take it up to her while she had to go upstairs. I took water up to her and then she never made any noise or anything. Next thing she called me again and I went back up and she said to go and take a piece of cloth that she had and put it on the stove until it gets brown and put it over his . . . she told me how far to cut the cord. Well, I tied a string around it and I cut it and then she told me to put the cloth on it so, which I did, and put a band around him. Oh, when he was born, she told me what to do to clean him up after something. Then I bathed him, wrapped him up, and she took him in and seemed like she nursed him right away. . . . I was in school and every time my mother would have a baby, she would say, "Get those girls to come in, I need them here." Then my dad would take [us] out of school. We never finished high school. We'd go home and help her with all those babies that she had. . . . With all the children she had, she didn't stay in bed. She got right up but she had us helping her around, you know. (1–2)

Ginny F. herself was in Browning when her four children were born:

I didn't have any trouble here. I just went to the hospital. . . . I had my first child when I was twenty-eight, very old. I had a hard time with my first baby because I was old, I guess. That is what they tell me. My second baby, I didn't have any trouble. There was no one to tell me how to feed them or anything . . . my mother was gone [deceased]. I didn't have anyone except the hospital and the nurse. . . . They used to keep us for ten days, when the babies were finished nursing, they would take them back to wherever they kept the babies. (1996, 1)

Asked whether her mother had told her about childbirth in the early reservation period, Ginny F. said:

Yes. She did say they had midwives in those days. They helped women out who I guess was having their babies. . . . I knew a midwife, she was my aunt but was no full-blood, her name was A. P. She used to go around and take care of them in the country. She would come and help my mother out. My aunt lived a little ways above, and my other aunt, M., they used to help each other out when they had their babies. Midwives, about four families were together and they would have their babies and then some of them would go and help out. None of them had any bad luck with anything. (1996, 2–3)

By the 1930s, appalling reservation mortality statistics fueled a move to bring medical services to Indians out of Bureau of Indian Affairs control and under the U.S. Public Health Service, enabled by Congress in 1954 (Prucha 1986, 353). Beginning in 1955, then, Indian women came under policies and practices formulated for the American population as a whole. The interviews I obtained from Pikuni women on the Blackfeet Reservation in 1996—and the interviews I did not obtain because several women would only exclaim, "It was terrible, a horror story! Unbelievably bad!"—held the same theme, the subordination of the women to the authority of the medical staff. It happened that the woman from whom I rented a kitchenette unit in Browning during that month of fieldwork wanted to participate in the project, so I recorded her experiences although she is not Indian. Her narrative of a Chicago working-class Irish-American paralleled those of the Pikuni women, alerting us to the social class relations framing the Indian women's lives as they do the Irish-American woman's. Politically, Indian reservations are Fourth World colonies, but pragmatically, most of their residents live in the circumstances of low socioeconomic class. The question is, does this subordination result from social class position vis-à-vis middle-class medical staff, or is there a broader context framing these experiences?

Interviewee Janet D. is a nurse, sixty years old in 1996, who has worked in the Indian hospital in Browning since 1957. Herself Pikuni and a lifelong resident of the reservation, Janet D. explained that under the Bureau of Indian Affairs Indian Health Service, the hospital did not permit the mother's family to enter the labor room:

> The father usually brought the mother to the hospital and the hospital received her and closed the door to the father, brought the expectant mother in and she went through labor by herself, usually never had a coach or never had even anybody with her except the doctor and a nurse and sometimes, we were lucky if there was a doctor attending. So her labor was alone and her delivery was usually with just the doctor and nurse in attendance. Usually you never saw the husband until about the next day after delivery. . . . I was really, really concerned because I was one of the nurses, you know, that according to hospital policy, closed the door of the hospital to the husband and the family and then they went back to the ranch or sometimes . . . just went downtown . . . and then heard his baby was born. (1996, 1)

Policy changed about 1960, Janet D. said:

> When the new hospital happened, we opened our wards a little bit more
> and were more open to caring for the family as well as the mother. . . . The
> new addition to the hospital caused an open ward situation and so there
> was really no way that we could lock doors anymore and so people, espe-
> cially moms and grandmoms and sisters, stayed with the mothers while
> they were in labor. (1996, 1)

Two factors operated here, the change in hospital design and the
underlying shift in societal attitudes that stimulated the design. Under the
U.S. Public Health Service, the reservation hospital more easily reflected
alterations in dominant U.S. values. It should be noted that although the
Browning Community Hospital is the only one on the reservation, there
is a public county hospital in the town of Cut Bank on the principal high-
way just east of the reservation, thirty-seven miles from Browning. Pikuni
women could use this hospital but would be required to pay for its services, whereas they were not charged for the use of the reservation facilities. Given the poverty and high unemployment on the reservation
throughout the twentieth century, few Pikuni women had any alternative
to the Browning hospital. Whether in this hospital or the rural county hospital, these women would be subordinated to the dominant society's scenarios for childbirth. As Janet D. testifies, no matter how sympathetic and
concerned the nurse might be toward traditional family attendance, staff
could not defy rules.

Janet D. is happy that conditions have improved:

> Attitudes started to include fathers more in the preparation and in the
> delivery. With the construction of the newer hospital, we have a family
> delivery room. I am excited when I hear that dads are going to Lamaze
> meetings or that dads are anxious to see the ultrasounds of their babies and
> are present during these times a lot of the time, and that this particular
> family unit [mother, father, and infant] is starting to come back together
> again. . . . So all in all, I think that things are starting to come back to where
> both parents are responsible for the birth of the baby. . . . Now within our
> family and within a lot of families, I know when my grandson was born
> down in Great Falls, we had every one of my children there and their chil-
> dren were there, and the nurse had to step over us. In this day and age, it's
> getting to be where it is quite a family celebration. So much family is

involved, and to be right there just for the instant and the time and all that but from what I can recall and from what little history I know, there has never been that excitement or celebration in a birth, . . . the joyfulness and the celebration of all that, that we experience today with a birth in our families. (1996, 2, 3, 4).

Janet D. laughed when the interviewer asked whether she had heard about the expectation that a Pikuni mother would be so distressed by her daughter's pain during labor that she couldn't bear to remain in the cabin with her. Then she elaborated:

Oh, I have actually seen it. And especially I think it is a mom in labor that is not tolerating the labor very well and doesn't know what is happening. I've seen in a couple of cases where the mom has actually went down, left the unit and went down to the waiting room, coming down the hall from the hospital just because they couldn't tolerate and they could still hear their daughter hollering. That has happened more than once. And I think I would, too, if I was the mom, knowing I couldn't do anything about it, I would leave the situation. So, yes, I can remember in particular, one mom and the daughter would say, "Ma! Ma!" and she would be yelling from down the hall and the mom would be way down the hall and say, "Oh, I can't stand to hear this." So, yeah, and that's just been in recent years, too. . . .

Husbands are the one that can do something because if they have been coached, I mean taught to coach, they say, and I've seen husband get more control of the situation than even the doctor or a nurse with the mom. Husband can come and say, "Now, knock that off, remember you got to get in control with your breathing." They come in a real coaching manner and a real partner in this thing and say, "Now, you don't have to do that, you don't have to yell, now breathe," and expectant moms are just, they do that, they listen to their husbands when they are in labor. I have seen that more than once. . . .

I know older women in our community, their concept of labor and delivery at that time was like, bite the bullet, you know. Bite the bullet or bite, I know there are a lot of times they bite washcloths and stuff, you know, for the pain. But there was no way that they could understand, you know, the muscles of the body and the relaxation of the muscles that would help. . . . They just felt like if they could get through a labor pain and then the next one, and the next one, then eventually it would be over with. But they couldn't see labor as being an event. You know, they looked at it as torture, just total torture. And could not understand what was going on. Whereas now, we teach our patients and they have more understanding to realize why you have to relax, why that cervix has to relax so that it can dilate, and all of this kind of stuff.

In regard to my children, I delivered four children, . . . my oldest is thirty-five now and . . . it was ten years from the oldest to the youngest. . . . My husband was kind of in the old thought, cowboy/rancher type dad that would just bring his wife in and leave her and come back and pick her up. So a lot of the labor and deliveries I had were alone. For my first couple, he was not that available. He was there to name them and see them at birth and stuff like that. But I just see my son who is a father of two, he never left those babies from the time, oh, I think from the time they were conceived until now, he's still training, potty training them and taking a real role of a dad, but he was very present in the delivery room. . . .

Your first delivery seems to be your hardest, and they had to do a spinal with me at that time and do forceps delivery. Of course, with my second delivery, it seemed to be pretty easy in regard to the child was in good position and I seemed to be well prepared. My husband was with me at that time. And then my third delivery, the baby was pretty big and her shoulders kind of . . . but you know, it was a case of do or die. I mean, they gave me the appropriate medication and I seemed to be able to tolerate everything well. And in my last delivery, my baby had to be incubated and had to be bagged a little bit because she had the cord around the neck and had some little problems there, but outside of that, I think most of my deliveries were pretty good, pretty hard labor but maybe I can't tolerate pain as well. But I feel like I was well prepared and had good coaches, and never alone unless I wanted to be. Sometimes there is a time when you like to be alone during labor, and of course, I had friendly physicians because they were all my friends who were working here and everything, and if I needed any kind of expert advice or care, it was always available even if we had to go a hundred miles for it. . . .

I've seen in regard to my professional life, I've seen child-bearing be very, very painful in some situations here when we don't have anesthesia, and some dangerous situations from moms, and I have seen some really, really poor preparation in regard to prenatal care and in regard to complications. Out where we're at, we have to get them on a helicopter quick or else hope we have a surgeon or an OB specialist, which sometimes we don't, but I'm sure they are striving to do that. Lately, we are having more obstetricians available to our people. . . . We have a Blackfoot doctor in labor and delivery, Dr. M. D., in fact, she's gone back for a residency in obstetrics so we definitely have young Dr. M. D., and she has got a lot of kids herself. She has gone through a lot of pregnancies so she is very, very good, very understanding, very well prepared to take care of the labor and delivery situations here.

So with that in mind, you see things [are] better than what they were, but I knew some of the older, I know my mom can tell me of a breech delivery that she had with my youngest sister and she just wanted to die. And the pain was so great that she just wanted to die. (1996, 2, 7, 8)

Commentary. Janet D. describes substantial changes in the attitudes concerning parturition for Pikuni on the Blackfeet Reservation. The traditional expectation, heard also in Insima's account, was that labor would be painful, only partially relieved through herbal brews and massage. Janet D. is an advocate for controlled breathing, coached by husband or friend, to battle pain by relaxation between contractions. She testifies not only concerning this significant shift in expectations, but also to the return of community to the labor room, once again husband, sisters, aunts, and—if she can stand the emotion—mother surrounding the parturient.

THE BUREAUCRATIC MACHINE AND THE PARTURIENT WOMAN

In 1918, Dakota medical doctor Charles Eastman lamented that the country's First Nations had "'fallen into the clutches of a Bureau Machine, which controls our property, our money, our children and our personal rights'" (Iverson 1982, 148). From the point of view of a commissioner of the Bureau of Indian Affairs, blame for the unhappy conditions on reservations must be borne by his superiors, the members of Congress: writing in 1892 to Senator Dawes, Commissioner Thomas Morgan passed on Dr. Carlos Montezuma's

pitiful appeal in behalf of the humane treatment of the unfortunate sick under his care [at Fort Stevenson, North Dakota]. . . . I have pleaded and urged and begged for money for hospitals, but have been refused, and I am helpless. . . . You may see how an Indian [Dr. Montezuma] looks at this matter and . . . may divide with me the sorrow, which I know you feel as well as I, that we must turn a deaf ear to such calls of humanity. (Iverson 1982, 20)

Dr. Eastman's term "the Bureau Machine" aptly conveys the inexorable power of a bureaucracy that seems to answer to no one. My Browning landlady reported that her daughter, married to a Blackfoot, complained of

> a total lack of compassion up here at the Indian Health Service for the pregnant women. . . . She thought they were very cold people when she'd go up there for her checkups or anything. She said she felt like she was another person in the assembly line. (Luann N. 1996, 3)

For nurse Janet D., coldness lay in the structure that obfuscated the staff's real compassion. Who or what created that structure?

Some simple answers can be discounted. Racism is certainly pervasive in Montana, but Luann's Irish-American daughter "felt like she was another person in the assembly line" (Luann N. 1996, 4) where non-Indians married into the Nation and Blackfeet who evidenced preponderantly non-Indian genetics were not differentiated from women who looked, and were known to be, preponderantly Pikuni. Nor is simple male dominance the answer; as this book demonstrates, women nurses and doctors have often been perceived to be "cold" and unresponsive. Most interesting, perhaps, is the testimony of this book that class status is not the answer—educated bourgeois parturients shared experiences of working-class and reservation women.

It must be made clear at this point that however similar the women's emotional responses may seem, Euro-American and European bourgeois women have not faced the drastic threats raised to women of the First Nations of America. Russell Thornton's *American Indian Holocaust and Survival* is not overly dramatically titled: women and children were deliberately gunned down by U.S. troops in a number of nineteenth-century massacres, and as late as the 1970s, a number of women claimed they were sterilized without their consent, or that "consent" was given under duress, in Indian Health Service hospitals (Jaimes and Halsey 1992, 326). (Sterilization was said to be a prophylactic measure for women judged by the doctor to have "enough" children. The birth rate per 1,000 women for American Indian women in 1964 was 43.3 per 1,000, versus 23.7 for the United States as a whole, and in 1970 it was 33 per 1,000, declining to 26.7 per 1,000 in 1980 versus 15.8 for the United States as a whole [Thornton 1987, 168].)

The extraordinary rate of un- and underemployment on reservations, as high as 80 percent,[3] contributes to frustration and bitterness that tend to boil over into drinking and violence, undermining women's efforts to care for their loved ones (Lopata 1994, 81; John 1988). From "civilizing" missions to benign neglect, schools and agencies dealing with reservations have naively promulgated the conquerors' propaganda that Indians are childlike primitives incapable of mature judgment, incompetent in contemporary economic endeavors, instinctively worshipping Nature. Women of the First Nations shoulder the burden of maintaining their nations' heritages as well as its physical survival.

MASTERS AND SUBJECTS

John Stuart Mill declared,

> the lot of the poor, in all things which affect them collectively, should be regulated for them, not by them. They should not be required or encouraged to think for themselves, or give to their own reflection or forecast an influential voice in the determination of their destiny. It is the duty of the higher classes to think for them, and to take the responsibility of their lot, as the commander and officers of an army take that of the soldiers composing it. . . . [W]hile yielding passive and active obedience to the rules prescribed for them, [the poor] may resign themselves in all other respects to a trustful insouciance, and repose under the shadow of their protectors . . . affectionate tutelage on the one side, respectful and grateful deference on the other. The rich should be in loco parentis to the poor, guiding and restraining them like children. Of spontaneous action on their part there should be no need. (cited in Newby 1977, 424–25)

Commenting on the contemporary workplace, Joan Acker (1991) notes that

> the manipulation and management of women's and men's sexuality, procreation, and emotion, are part of the control processes of organizations, maintaining not only gender stratification but also contributing to maintaining class and . . . race and ethnic relations. . . . The abstract job, devoid of a human body, is a basic unit in such systems of control. (175)

Parallel to the rational-technical image of jobs is the abstracted citizen, until (and in many localities in the United States well after) the 1920s a male Euro-American. The U.S. Constitution was not construed to have meant "man" generically, but literally; it explicitly excluded enslaved men from citizenship, and the Congress de facto excluded American Indian men by dealing with their nations through treaties, as foreign sovereign powers, although after two generations the United States felt itself militarily strong enough to reduce them to the strange status of "domestic dependent nations," their members to be treated as wards. Recognized American Indians then shared this status with women and the poor.

What women as a class and American Indians as a class have shared is subordination to a governing class drawn from literate, English-speaking, Euro-American men. American Indians, as a class, gained the right to vote as citizens four years after American women gained suffrage. Before the 1920s, both American Indians and women, as classes, had the legal status of minors, their finances and conduct subject to decisions made for them by white men. Conventionally, such circumstances are termed "patriarchy," but the feminist scholar Elisabeth Schüssler Fiorenza (1994) introduces the better term "kyriarchy" (14), meaning rule by lords/masters. A kyriarchic society is strongly hierarchical. It tends to "naturalize" its structure of rule by invoking the metaphor of family, equating the lord/master with a father and those he rules with the supposedly weak and foolish wife and children. Schüssler Fiorenza points out, tellingly, that in kyriarchal societies only men of the exclusive dominant class exercise paternal power, emasculating (sometimes literally) fathers of the disenfranchised classes; hence *patriarchy* is a misleading label.

Pikuni have been brought up in a culture that disrespects and resists lordly behavior, a society in which people voted with their feet, abandoning men who have tried to command rather than consult. In the Pikuni world, there are leaders but no masters. Traditional leaders have been generous and diplomatic, cultivating their followers' confidence rather than exerting domination. Individual autonomy, not ascribed positions, is the basic political principle (Kehoe 1995), and this political structure has been congruent with an ecology, the Northwestern Plains, low in resource density and therefore low in human population.

Sun-Lights-Her-Pipe, a Pikuni a generation older than Insima, was a model leader:

> Her countenance was feminine, but with the stamp of leadership. Her carriage was graceful but always expressing dignity. "Mother-of-all" was her real name and appropriate, it seemed to me, expressing in a measure the veneration in which she was held by her neighbors. . . . Her soft deep voice

added [to the] . . . grace and fine manners after the way of her people. . . . She began, speaking slowly and in well-formed sentences, saying that it made her old eyes glad to see many people here, so many happy faces, . . . people so well-dressed, such an abundance of food for the feast, also the many quilts, moccasins, robes, etc., piled up ready for distribution at the "give-away" to accompany this ceremony. . . . She prayed to[ward] the sun for . . . all the people assembled (Wissler 1971, 279–89). [Note: prayers are directed toward the sun as the visible manifestation of Almighty Power.]

Her age, health, and relative prosperity proved that her exemplary character had earned her approbation from the Almighty. She and her equally respected husband abjured the overbearing, demanding attitude Westerners might accept from men in commanding positions. Schüssler Fiorenza would find many on the reservation who agree that the commanding class is a kyriarchy, not a class of fathers.

There has grown, in recent years, a body of research and discussion on the situations of colonized peoples. Proliferating, these studies begin to illustrate that the downtrodden, disenfranchised subaltern colonized are indeed frequently subject to the legal status and patronizing rule suffered by women of the imperial nations; these studies bring out, also, that the common metaphor of patriarchy, the supposedly benevolent domination by Fathers urged by Mill, elides disparate situations and unexpected alliances (Foley et al. 1995; Thapar 1995, 107). The Bengali writer Ashis Nandy (1983) appropriately takes the subaltern's standpoint in dissecting the colonizers' assumption that the conquered are simultaneously, conflictingly "childlike" and "childish": "childlike" in being "innocent, ignorant but willing to learn . . . 'corrigible'" and "childish" in being "ignorant but unwilling to learn, ungrateful, sinful, savage, unpredictably violent, disloyal and, thus, 'incorrigible'" (16). Under Nandy's distinction, Western women would be conventionally looked upon (by the dominant men) as "childlike," while American Indians were "childish." Yet look at standard American obstetrical practice (Rothman 1982, 30; Rothman 1989, 53; Jordan 1993, 86, 112–13), the parturient woman stripped, immobilized by leather straps, her pubic area shaved, electronic monitors attached to her body, "coached" because it is assumed she is helplessly out of control. (I know from my own experience that a few minutes of someone guiding one's breathing rhythm can really help the parturient woman; what I decry is the assumption that she is bound to be out of control, that she cannot know and ask just when those few minutes will be helpful, that she must be constantly coached.) Surely this practice drops the American woman into the class of "childish" subjects who must, as Nandy observed, be "repressed" rather than "taught" (16).

The critical element linking American women and American Indians, both men and women, is the creation of Other by the dominant class of (European/Euro-American) men. Susanne Zantop (1997), in a study of German ideology precursory to the actual colonizations of the Bismarck era, suggests the following:

> From the safe distance of the [European] province, and from the safe distance of the disinterested theorist, "natural philosophers" devise strategies for creating order and dispelling myths. By colonizing irrational fantasies and organizing them into seemingly rational structures, these theories not only define and contain a threatening or alluring "other"—but invent a self, which is male, white, and ["European"] (45; I have changed her "German" to "European," which does not change her meaning).

If the writer's self is conceived as male, white, and European, his Other must be feminine—woman or childlike, emasculated—and racially distinct. To support this ideological construct, in 1885 there was published, to immediate and long-lasting popularity, *Das Weib*, subtitled *The Natural History of Woman*. Readers of the many editions of this tome, for which there was a three-volume English translation as late as 1935 (Weideger 1986, 13–17), were instructed that women, like savages, are irrational, improvident, fickle, sensual, and swayed by Nature rather than Reason. Thus the class of women was merged with non-Europeans destined to be colonized, never mind a woman's white skin color and European (or Euro-American) birthplace. Into this same capacious class went European peasants, men and women, *Landeskinder* benevolently ruled by their aristocratic *Landesvater* (Zantop 1997, 154). By 1939, Germans were told that "just as children piously and full of trust surrender themselves to the protection of their father, venerating him and yet feeling close to him as his children, so our natives approach, free and easy, the Führer" (Zantop 1997, 201).

Perhaps it seems too extreme, perhaps tasteless, to allude to the most evil white male European to make the point that the kyriarch may be persuaded of his own benevolence, but those upon whom his will is imposed may think otherwise, and not irrationally. In North America, during the century 1870–1970, Euro-American women and American

Indians struggled, in parallel domains, to be acknowledged legally competent adults, to be allowed political rights, to be listened to and enabled to make decisions on their own affairs. The two Pikuni women who couldn't bear to recount their experiences giving birth both have achieved professional status on the reservation; neither woman wanted to bring to mind the contrast between the position of responsibility she now enjoys and the helplessness she felt—was supposed to feel—while in labor. As Mill declared, "Of spontaneous action on their part there should be no need; respectful and grateful deference" is proper on the part of the laboring classes toward their "protectors" (cited in Newby 1977, 424–25).

Laura R. (1996) helped her sister, "just keeping her in the moment, talking to her and massaging her that kept her stimulated, you know, and into the moment until what was happening" (2). "Keeping her in the moment," "talking to her," keeping her "stimulated," Laura R. refuted the kyriarchy's rational-technical definition of parturience as a "job," confounded its tutelage that the woman, poor, be mute, passive, obedient to the authority figure. Bringing her the root known to Blackfoot midwives, Laura R. asserted the medical knowledge of the Pikuni world, parallel to kyriarchal medical orthodoxy. Reliance on "sisters"—in Blackfoot terminology, female siblings and cousins—for assistance in childbirth, led by a trained and experienced midwife, if one was close enough to attend, was the best means toward successful childbirth in Blackfoot country. After motor transport to hospitals became available, kyriarchal American birth practices could be endorsed by the Indian Health Service and agency officials. The "cold" professional manner stemming from the kyriarchy's rational-technical ideology ignored women's humanity, a stance worsened in the generally poorly-staffed Indian Health Service hospitals; still, in the hospital a woman was less likely to die, as had Ginny F.'s mother.

Mitigation of kyriarchal structure and ideology in American society since the 1960s can be seen both in the incorporation of fathers and families in hospitals' labor rooms (Davis-Floyd 1993, 143–46) and in the tremendous upheavals carried out as affirmative action, civil rights enforcement, disability provisions, and casual-dress styles. On Indian reservations, this trend is abundantly visible in decentralization of the "Bureau Machine," control of education and reservation funds shifted to the tribal governments, and a resurgence of native languages and religious practices (Kehoe 1992, 584–92). Since the 1920s, Pikuni women's birthing experiences have been similar to those of their fellow American citizens. The

colonial situation of reservation women brings into sharper focus the status of First World women, for generations classed with "the poor" and
American Indians as "an ignorant and dependent race" owing respectful
and grateful deference to the masters of the kyriarchy.

NOTES

1. The following are pseudonyms for women whose interviews are cited in this chapter:

   1. Insima: Transcription of interviews, 1939, focusing on early reservation period
   (1880s to 1890s);
   2. Mrs. Ginny F.: Woman in her nineties describing also her mother's generation
   (same as Insima's);
   3. Mrs. Janet D.: Nurse at Indian Health Service hospital;
   4. Mrs. Laura R.: Young woman studying at Blackfeet Community College;
   5. Luann N.: Irish Catholic working-class woman from Chicago.
   Excerpts from interview with Cecile Sanderville Yellow-Wolf Yellow-Kidney (I'nssimaa)
   by Sue Sommers (Dietrich), August, 1939, Blackfeet Reservation, Montana.

   Note that I'nssimaa (born 1869) is written as Insima or Insema; Agnes Chief-All-
   Over (born 1882) is I'nssimaa's daughter, who was interpreting.
2. The Southern Piegan, *Pikuni* in Blackfoot, are one of the four groups of the
   Blackfoot alliance. They occupied north-central Montana in the nineteenth century
   and were allotted their present reservation in 1874. The other three groups are the
   Blood (Kainai), North Peigan (Pikuni), and Blackfoot proper (Siksika), all settled
   on reserves in Alberta just north of the U.S. border.
      Sources on Blackfoot include DeMarce 1980; Ewers 1955, 1958; Farr 1984;
   Goldfrank 1945; Graham 1979; Ground 1978; Hanks and Hanks 1945, 1950;
   Kehoe 1976, 1983, 1993; Lewis 1941, 1942; McClintock [1910] 1968; McFee 1972;
   Rides At The Door 1979; Uhlenbeck 1911, 1912; Wissler 1911, 1912, [1938] 1971;
   and Wissler and Duvall 1908.
3. Official figures for unemployment are based on persons actively seeking or recently
   released from participation in the labor force. The 1990 U.S. Census reported that
   32.6 percent of "core" American Indians (self-reported to be of the Indian "race"
   and Indian ancestry) were not in the labor force, and about the same percentage
   were to be classed as living in poverty (Nagle 1996, 98). Unemployment was officially recorded as more than 50 percent on many reservations in 1985 (Knack and
   Littlefield 1996, 24); this does not include underemployment, which is common.

REFERENCES

Acker, J. 1991. Hierarchies, jobs, bodies: A theory of gendered organizations.
    In *The social construction of gender*, ed. J. Lorber and S. A. Farrell, 162–79.
    Newbury Park, Calif.: Sage.

Davis-Floyd, R. 1993. Update. In *Birth in four cultures,* 4th ed., ed. R. Davis-Floyd, 143–46. Prospect Heights, Ill.: Waveland Press.

DeMarce, R., ed. 1980. *Blackfeet heritage, 1907–1908.* Browning, Mont.: Blackfeet Heritage Program

Ewers, J. C. 1955. The horse in Blackfoot Indian culture. In Smithsonian Institution *Bureau of American Ethnology Bulletin 159.* Washington: Government Printing Office.

———. 1958. *The Blackfeet: Raiders on the northwestern plains.* Norman: University of Oklahoma Press.

Farr, W. E. 1984. *The reservation Blackfeet, 1882–1945.* Seattle: University of Washington Press.

Foley, T. P., L. Pilkington, S. Ryder, and E. Tilley. 1995. Introduction. In *Gender and colonialism,* ed. T. P. Foley, L. Pilkington, S. Ryder, and E. Tilley, 8–11. Galway: Galway University Press.

Ginny F. 1996. Interview by Alice Kehoe, 1 May. Available from Memorial Library Archives, Marquette University, Milwaukee, WI 53201.

Goldfrank, E. S. 1945. *Changing configurations in the social organization of a Blackfoot tribe during the reserve period (the Blood of Alberta, Canada).* Monograph 8, American Ethnological Society. Seattle: University of Washington Press.

Graham, J. D. (Schultz). 1979. In the lodge of the Matokiks: The women's buffalo society of the Blood Indians. In *Lifeways of intermontane and plains Montana Indians,* ed. L. B. Davis, 27–32. Occasional Papers of the Museum of the Rockies, No. 1. Bozeman: Montana State University.

Ground, M. 1978. *Grass Woman stories.* Browning, Mont.: Blackfeet Heritage Program.

Hanks, L. M., Jr., and J. R. Hanks. 1945. *Observations on Northern Blackfoot kinship.* Monograph 9, American Ethnological Society. Seattle: University of Washington Press.

———. 1950. *Tribe under trust: A study of the Blackfoot reserve of Alberta.* Toronto: University of Toronto Press.

Harrod, H. L. 1971. *Mission among the Blackfeet.* Norman: University of Oklahoma Press.

Hungry Wolf, B. 1982. *The ways of my grandmothers.* New York: Quill.

Insima. 1939. Interview by Sue Sommers (Dietrich), August, trans. Agnes Chief-All-Over. Available from Memorial Library Archives, Marquette University, Milwaukee, WI 53201.

Iverson, P. 1982. *Carlos Montezuma and the changing world of American Indians.* Albuquerque: University of New Mexico Press.

Jaimes, M. A., and T. Halsey. 1992. American Indian women. In *The state of Native America*, M. A. Jaimes, 311–44. Boston: South End Press.

Janet D. 1996. Interview by Alice Kehoe, 29 April. Available from Memorial Library Archives, Marquette University, Milwaukee, WI 53201.

John, R. 1988. The Native American family. In *Ethnic families in America*, 3d ed., ed. C. H. Mindel, R. W. Habenstein, and R. Wright Jr., 325–63. New York: Elsevier.

Jordan, B. 1993. *Birth in four cultures.* 4th ed. Robbie Davis-Floyd. Prospect Heights, Ill.: Waveland Press.

Kehoe, A. B. 1976. Old woman had great power. *Western Canadian Journal of Anthropology* 6:68–76.

———. 1983. The shackles of tradition. In *The hidden half*, ed. P. Albers and B. Medicine, 53–73. Washington, D.C.: University Press of America.

———. 1992. *North American Indians: A comprehensive account.* 2d ed. Englewood Cliffs, N.J.: Prentice Hall.

———. 1993. How the ancient Peigans lived. *Research in Economic Anthropology* 14:87–105.

———. 1995. Blackfoot persons. In *Women and power in Native America*, ed. L. F. Klein and L. A. Ackerman, 113–25. Norman: University of Oklahoma Press.

———. 1996. Transcribing Insima, a Blackfoot "old lady." In *Reading beyond words: Native history in context*, ed. J. S. H. Brown and E. Vibert, 381–402. Orchard Park, N.Y.: Broadview Press.

Knack, M. C., and A. Littlefield. 1996. Native American labor. In *Native Americans and wage labor*, ed. A. Littlefield and M. C. Knack, 3–44. Norman: University of Oklahoma Press.

Laura R. 1996. Interview by Alice Kehoe, 2 May. Available from Memorial Library Archives, Marquette University, Milwaukee, WI 53201.

Lewis, O. 1941. Manly-hearted women among the North Piegan. *American Anthropologist* 43:173–87.

———. 1942. *The effects of white contact upon Blackfoot culture.* Monograph 6, American Ethnological Society. Seattle: University of Washington Press.

Lopata, H. Z. 1994. *Circles and settings.* Albany: State University of New York Press.

Luann N. 1996. Inteview by Alice Kehoe, 2 May. Available from Memorial Library Archives, Marquette University, Milwaukee, WI 53201.

McClintock, W. 1968. *The old north trail.* Lincoln: University of Nebraska Press. Reprinted from *The old north trail*, by W. McClintock, London: Macmillan, 1910.

McFee, M. 1972. *Modern Blackfeet: Montanans on a reservation.* New York: Holt, Rinehart & Winston.

Nagle, J. 1996. *American Indian ethnic renewal.* New York: Oxford University Press.

Nandy, A. 1983. *The intimate enemy: Loss and recovery of self under colonialism.* Delhi: Oxford University Press.

Newby, H. 1977. *The deferential worker.* London: Allen Lane.

Prucha, F. P. 1986. *The Great Father.* Abridged ed. Lincoln: University of Nebraska Press.

Rides At The Door, D. D. 1979. *Napi stories.* Browning, Mont.: Blackfeet Heritage Program.

Rothman, B. K. 1982. *In labor: Women and power in the birthplace.* New York: W. W. Norton.

———. 1989. *Recreating motherhood: Ideology and technology in a patriarchal society.* New York: W. W. Norton.

Schüssler Fiorenza, E. 1994. *Jesus: Miriam's child, Sophia's prophet: Critical issues in feminist christology.* New York: Continuum.

Thapar, S. 1995. *The marginalization of women in writings on the Indian nationalist movement.* In *Gender and colonialism,* ed. T. P. Foley, L. Pilkington, S. Ryder, and E. Tilley, 103–23. Galway: Galway University Press.

Thornton, R. 1987. *American Indian holocaust and survival.* Norman: University of Oklahoma Press.

Uhlenbeck, C. C. 1911. Original Blackfoot texts, Verhandelingen der Koninklijke Akademie van Wetenschappen te Amsterdam, Afdeeling Letterkunde n. r. 12 (1). Amsterdam: Johannes Muller.

———. 1912. A new series of Blackfoot texts, Verhandelingen der Koninklijke Akademie van Wetenschappen te Amsterdam, Afdeeling Letterkunde n. r. 13 (1). Amsterdam: Johannes Muller.

Weideger, P. 1986. *History's mistress.* Harmondsworth, England: Penguin.

Wissler, C. 1911. The social life of the Blackfoot Indians. *Anthropological Papers* 7:1–64. New York: American Museum of Natural History.

———. 1912. Ceremonial bundles of the Blackfoot Indians. *Anthropological Papers* 7:65–289. New York: American Museum of Natural History.

———. 1971. *Red man reservations.* New York: Collier. Original work published 1938 as *Indian cavalcade or life on the old-time Indian reservations,* New York: Sheridan House.

Wissler, C., and D. C. Duvall. 1908. Mythology of the Blackfoot Indians, *Anthroplogical Papers* 2:1–163. New York: American Museum of Natural History.

Zantop, S. 1997. *Colonial fantasies: Conquest, family, and nation in precolonial Germany, 1770–1870.* Durham, N.C.: Duke University Press.

5

CONTROL VERSUS RECIPROCITY
A Nurse/Midwife Perspective

Leona VandeVusse

ost births in the United States occur in hospitals and are attended by physicians. In most other countries, midwives attend the majority of normal births (Rooks 1997). Davis-Floyd (1986, 1992), Mitford (1992), and others have critiqued the American hospital environment for its culture of technocracy. Technocracy is a belief system that insists technology improves upon nature (Davis-Floyd 1992), with *technology* in the case of birth referring to provider-ordered equipment, such as electronic fetal monitors, as well as to provider-determined interventions that affect the course of labor, such as insisting that women remain in bed. In a culture of technocracy, the use of technology is viewed as normal and is expected in all labors; it is seen not only as improving births but as being essential to the health and safety of infants and mothers. Yet to my mind, this critique of technology, while important, avoids discussions of the real issue: control.

As a certified nurse-midwife who researches women's birth narratives, I believe that control over women is a salient issue, if not *the* salient issue, in birth and its outcomes, regardless of technology use. Therefore, I find it useful to talk not so much about the culture of technocracy as about the culture of control. Within the culture of control, consumers and professionals share the following set of assumptions: One, providers know more about birth than the women experiencing it. Two, providers are the ones who should make decisions about the use of technology and other interventions. And three, because providers are regarded as professionals who have had more education and a wider variety of experiences attending births, they and the system that supports them should not be questioned. This culture of control is increasingly problematic the more it excludes the women from participating in decision making about their own bodies.

Consequently, I believe that the culture of control should be replaced with a culture of reciprocity. A culture of reciprocity occurs when consumers and professionals share the following beliefs: One, the natural processes of birth are complex, interrelated events that work best together without interference. Two, because natural processes of birthing are respected and trusted, technology use and other interventions should be limited to the small number of situations in which they are needed to handle a problem; in normal births, professionals should wait, observe, and provide supportive care. And three, consumers and professionals should share the decision making. To demonstrate in this chapter why a culture of control should be replaced with a culture of reciprocity, I first critique the technocratic culture of control, then I employ women's own stories as the grounds for defining a culture of reciprocity and for discovering the implications of such a culture for caregivers.

CRITIQUING TECHNOLOGY DURING BIRTH

Different worldviews about childbirth have been summarized by Wagner (1994) during his international work to improve birth care. As a former officer of the World Health Organization and a pediatrician and perinatal epidemiologist, Wagner sponsored large, multidisciplinary consensus conferences in Europe and South America. These conferences involved professionals and laypeople from the local communities, examining the circumstances and outcomes of birth in their countries. According to Wagner, there were two major outlooks on birth at these conferences: the medical and the social. Proponents of the medical view focused primarily on biological aspects of birth and worked to control its unpredictability with technology. Those espousing the social view recognized the wider context of human interactions with the environment and worked to limit technology to interfere least with family and cultural issues. Wagner acknowledged that there was conflict between these two views regarding the application of technology for birth. He also noted their common goal: healthy mothers and infants. He then suggested that these two views could be complementary, concluding that decisions about the conduct of birth in a country should be made by a wide array of interested individuals and groups, not predominantly professionals.

Much research has been done debunking the notion that high technology use protects mothers and infants who have a normal labor and birth. For example, Enkin et al. (2000) and Goer (1995), among others, have summarized a large body of research about childbirth. These authors represent different specialties; they are primarily physicians and epidemiologists but include interested consumers and childbirth educators. Using the strongest standard for discriminating significant differences in research—that is, randomized controlled trials (RCTs)—the researchers attempted to reduce bias by randomly assigning people to various groups. Controlled conditions attempted to reduce the number of interferences that could alter the results and make interpretation more difficult. The groups were treated similarly except for one major difference, and the results were then compared. Significant differences could thus be attributed to the differential treatment of each particular group rather than to chance, individual variations, or bias in the design. Enkin et al. and Goer reviewed the evidence from much of the birth research, particularly RCTs done on various technologies and interventions. They concluded that much of the technology used in normal labor and birth has resulted in worsened outcomes or no improvement. The authors generally recommended avoiding technology and a variety of other interventions that interfere with the natural processes.

In addition, the Technical Working Group of the World Health Organization (WHO) examined many studies done by researchers throughout the world who have investigated procedures applied during labor and birth. They published their report (1997) on care in normal birth, which occurs for the majority of women. They used the term *normal birth* to include situations in which spontaneous onset of labor occurred at term with a healthy mother and a healthy fetus who was in the head-down position. The term was not meant to include the much smaller number of women who developed medical complications that were incompatible with such a birth. In general, the WHO group advocated using the least intervention possible that was compatible with safety.

According to the WHO group, one well-documented example of technology that was widely used but not required in the normal course of labor was continuous electronic fetal monitoring (EFM)—that is, using a machine to record contractions and fetal heart rate. According to Goer (1995) and others (Thacker and Stroup 2000), several large RCTs over a ten-year period consistently demonstrated that continuous EFM effected no difference in neonatal outcomes. The only significant difference documented for continuous EFM was a higher rate of cesarean sections, a negative effect. Despite research evidence, the practice of continuous EFM has remained in wide use, applied indiscriminately to normal laboring women as well as to those with risk factors. For example, Albers and Savitz (1991) analyzed a large national probability sample of data from American hospitals. They found that more technology was used for low-risk women in hospitals where more technology was available. These low-risk women were otherwise clinically similar to women in hospitals with less available technology. This unnecessary use of technology was not associated with benefits in outcomes. Therefore, these data suggest that the women received excessive technological interventions (particularly EFM) that were not based on identification of women's differing clinical needs but on the availability of medical technology in the environment.

Despite the fact that many women still routinely receive continuous EFM during labor, there is growing evidence in the practice-oriented literature for the superiority of less intervention. According to Supplee and Vezeau (1996), professional organizations have officially recommended a lower technology alternative for monitoring the woman and fetus periodically throughout labor: intermittent auscultation (IA), or listening to the fetal heart rate with a stethoscope at certain intervals. Based on reviews of multinational research results, including RCTs on many different procedures, the WHO group published guidelines for care in normal birth. The group members categorized practices that were shown to be useful, harmful, effective, or ineffective. They intended to discourage providers from using practices that were harmful to birth, while encouraging beneficial ones. They determined that continuous EFM was frequently and inappropriately used, and they supported IA as one practice with demonstrated usefulness that should be encouraged.

As a consumer (mother) and a certified nurse-midwife who has cared for many women during pregnancy, labor, and birth, I agree with the critiques of and conclusions about the technocratic approach to birth, which were made by sociologists, anthropologists, and others, both in the United States and internationally. I believe that routine use of technology in normal birth is unnecessary and can have harmful effects. When a decision is made that technology is needed, it would be best to have consciously analyzed the situation and included all involved people in the decision. This would reduce routine applications of technology.

ANALYZING WOMEN'S BIRTH STORIES: THE LINK BETWEEN DECISION MAKING AND CONTROL

This chapter is based on my research analyzing women's birth stories that were gathered in the early 1990s. A few of the births reported by the women had occurred in the late 1970s, but most had occurred in the late 1980s. These birth stories will, in the future, be available through the Birthing Project Archive at Marquette University.

In my study, a sample of women living in the Midwest were encouraged to express their birth stories in any way they wished. I did not ask the women for specific information about their births. The study informants spoke clearly, articulated exactly what they wanted to say, and ordered the events as they wished. They were equally definitive about when they were done. I audiotaped the birth stories of fifteen women, including women with multiple stories because they had more than one child. All told, there were thirty-three birth stories. All of the women had had a child within the three and a half months prior to being interviewed, and some had had their first child as many as fifteen years prior to being interviewed. Simkin (1991) demonstrated in a study of former students in her childbirth classes that women have good recall of their births, even twenty years after the event. I selectively chose the women participants to reflect a maximum diversity of experiences. I analyzed the verbatim transcriptions for the women's personal meanings of control, defined as the exercise of restraint or direction over, or holding back or in check (Stein and Su, 1980). The data were aggregated around all the birth stories; the unit of analysis was any expression of control in birth stories. The data were not analyzed in terms of individual women because during our discussions of informed consent I promised the women confidentiality.

The methods I used to analyze the birth narratives included the following: (a) content analysis for words and phrases, (b) thematic analysis for recurrent concepts, vignettes, and clusters of common experiences, and ultimately (c) interpretive statements that represented distillations of the women's meanings across the narratives. During my analysis, I carefully noted the nouns, verbs, and direct objects of the women's sentences, indicating the controlling agent, the controlling act, and the recipient of control, respectively. I also noted the vignettes embedded in the narratives about the women's experiences, vignettes that signified issues of control.

In addition to my own analyses, a group of coders from various disciplines, such as psychology, education, and business, assisted me by bringing unique perspectives to the analyses. They contributed to the depth and breadth of analysis, enhancing my own views. The coders were especially helpful in identifying conclusion statements (distillations of meanings) that were common across the women's stories.

WOMEN'S VIEWS ON CONTROL

It is important to establish that the women identified themselves and their bodily functions as agents of control throughout the stories. Yet the women reported that other people controlled aspects of their birth experiences much more frequently than the women themselves or the women's bodily functions acted as agents of control. When the women expressed how they exerted their own agency, they generally provided examples of the prenatal preparation they had undertaken, such as childbirth education classes and readying the household for the coming infant. They generally spoke with pride about the details to which they had attended. Similarly, the women identified their bodily functions, such as contractions and hormonally mediated responses like limb twitching, as exerting control during their labors and births.

The women, however, identified numerous other influences of control in their birth experiences. These influences of control included support people, other women in labor or recovery at the same time, and mass media–derived expectations. Yet the most frequently identified agents of control were other people—that is, the providers (including nurses, physicians, and midwives), childbirth educators, and even office staff. Of these, the ones who exerted the most control were those attending the women in labor and birth—the physicians, nurses, and midwives. It is important to note that the women did not convey that nurses, midwives, or physicians all responded in the same manner. The women acknowledged different provider styles in their birth stories.

The women often reported that providers exerted control through the application of various procedures. Many women indicated that provider control was an important issue for them. The women indicated this importance by their expression of emotions during the interview, the length of time they spent describing the event, and the words they chose to relay strong feelings. For example, women in this study identified EFM as one of several major ways that care providers exercised control over them. One woman reported that, although she had discussed her request not to be monitored with her care provider in advance of labor, EFM was used. She stated the care provider convinced her that monitoring was necessary during labor.

> I mean, we had talked all this over before . . . and she agreed to everything that I had wanted, but then, at the time of the birth, actually, things were

a little bit different then than I had authored. But . . . I was stuck in that bed because of the monitor being there.

This woman accurately identified one of the criticisms of using EFM: limited mobility for the women, once monitored. Ambulation is a no-technology intervention that has been shown to be beneficial for labor progress, but as this woman stated, she was "stuck" in the bed.

Another woman reported that she was told to use the bedpan instead of going to the bathroom because she had received analgesia and had continuous EFM. The first time she had to use the bedpan, she reported that she told her partner to leave the room. She stated that she was upset, but she was able to urinate into the bedpan. The second time, she told the nurse that she had to have a bowel movement and wanted to get up to use the toilet. The nurse explained both times that there was a need to continuously monitor the fetus; therefore the woman had to remain in bed.

> I said "Why? I can take the cords with me" and they wouldn't let me. I had to use a bedpan. And that upset me. . . . Then [a few hours later] I really had to go to the bathroom. I had to have a bowel movement, I knew that. . . . I said . . ."I have to go to the bathroom." . . . She said "Okay, fine, you can go. I'll get the bedpan." I said "No. I have to, you have to let me get up." And they said "No, we can't let you." . . . I tried to explain that I knew I was gonna have a bowel movement. "Please, let me go." "No." And so, after not being able to hold it and not being able to argue any longer, I said, "Okay, [Partner], you have to leave the room." They put the bedpan in. I had to have a bowel movement so I had to sit up. Meantime, the IV is getting all messed up, the blood is coming through the tubes. I mean, like, why don't you just let, I'm crying. "Just let me go to the bathroom." "No." They wouldn't let me, because, I don't know, they felt the baby's heartbeat was . . . going down or something, or mine. I don't know why. But I couldn't come off the monitors, and, so I had to sit myself up. Meantime, like I said, every time I moved caused a contraction, so irregardless, I had to sit up to have the bowel movement in the bedpan. I succeeded in getting it out . . . in total embarrassment, and the nurse is there. . . . I'm crying. . . . I was so embarrassed because I could feel my water breaking now, and the bedpan I knew was full. And I thought if I moved wrong it's going to go all over the bed. And she said "Don't worry, don't worry." And I was just crying, in tears, and she had to wipe me. I was so, I cried, I said "this wouldn't have happened if you

had just let me go to the bathroom on my own." So she [the nurse] got everything got under control.

Clearly, care providers sometimes acted as agents of control by using procedures that not only bothered but humiliated the women. The use of EFM limited the women's mobility and ability to carry out normal functions of daily living. After reviewing the scientific research evidence, the WHO group (1997) categorized freedom of movement throughout labor as a demonstrably useful practice that should be encouraged. The group also categorized EFM as a practice that was frequently used inappropriately. The women quoted in this study appeared to agree. In the examples noted, they reported emotions such as feeling stuck and being embarrassed and angry at the controls that were exerted over them and their activities.

WOMEN'S VIEWS ON DECISION MAKING

Control issues are inextricably related to patterns of decision making, for decisions always include questions of "who decides?" and "who does not?" as well as "who has the power to implement decisions?" and "who does not?" Consequently, an analysis of control in women's birth narratives must include an analysis of decision-making patterns. I therefore analyzed the women's birth narratives to identify specific types of decision making, and I discovered four major categories: (1) unilateral and uncontested or agreed upon; (2) contested but unilateral; (3) shared; and (4) suspended (waiting when unsure). Two types may be further subdivided. In unilateral but contested decision making, the person contesting the plan could eventually adapt to or refuse the decision. In shared decision making, the participants could make the decision by using explanations or by making requests. Therefore, a total of six ways in which control is exerted via decision making emerge from the birthing narratives. These six categories are summarized for easy reference in table 1 and then further explained in this section. These data have also been presented as a model in which decision making control is related along a continuum to the emotions women expressed in their birth stories (VandeVusse 1999a).

TABLE 1. CATEGORIES OF MEANS OF CONTROL THROUGH METHODS OF DECISION MAKING

MEANS OF CONTROL	METHOD OF DECISION MAKING
1. Unilateral and uncontested	1. Through agreement
2. Contested but unilateral	2a. Through eventual adaptation
	2b. Through eventual refusal
3. Shared	3a. Through use of explanations
	3b. Through making requests
4. Suspended (waited when unsure)	4. No active decision made

UNILATERAL AND UNCONTESTED CONTROL: DECISION MAKING THROUGH AGREEMENT

The first means of decision making as an indicator of control was when a unilateral decision was made by the care provider. It was uncontested by the woman, who complied with the provider's decision. For example, one woman reported having had a non-stress test without her explicit consent. She completed the test rather than objecting to it:

> . . . I didn't have a say in [the non-stress test], . . . I was kind of a little bit shocked. 'Cuz I went in the office and they just hooked me up. And I thought, hmm. But it's really, and I kind of rationalized, well, I'm going to lay here for this. It's really only kind of like ultrasound, you know, it's all right. So she [the physician] wants to do a stress test, okay. It turned out everything was fine on that.

In this case, the woman complied with the provider's decision and was ultimately satisfied because everything turned out fine. One senses, however, that she was not completely pleased with the ultrasound exposure since she commented on her need to rationalize it during the interview.

Another woman associated provider unilateral decision making with the high cesarean section rates that occur in hospitals. When she contrasted her hospital cesarean sections with her vaginal birth after cesarean (VBAC) at home with a lay-midwife, she was very clear that she could maintain control at home.

> I could not have stepped in a hospital and had the same experience. I would have felt that I had surrendered to them again. Here I am, you

know, 'cuz you have to, there's a certain amount of giving in you have to do when you sign away that you're in their care. And I didn't want to be in anybody's care. I was in my own care. . . . If I give up my being in charge about birth and they take over, it would have been their way. It might have been a cesarean. . . . I used the word "surrender" maybe a little bit too free and easy. But to me, it meant that I would be here, here I am, you know, I'm here to have a baby. Maybe you could do it for me. You know, you have before. 'Cuz when you have a cesarean, you don't really give birth. You have major surgery. Major abdominal surgery. And someone hands you a baby a few hours later, and says "here's your baby." Having a cesarean, and having that gift of womanhood taken away. . . . I had to do it on my own. I had to be in charge. But when it came to this birth, I wanted it to be my way at home. And I, I think I'd set out to do that, and we accomplished it. We're not ignorant of the medical field and what they stand for. They have a right to be there, and they're there for the people who need them to be. In my case, I didn't need them. So, they hold their place in the medical, you know, their place in society is fine. But where I was, what I had to accomplish, and where I had to go, I didn't need that part of the medical field. That was the way I was going to give birth. That was the *only way* I was going to give birth. Myself.

This woman reported that normally she was easygoing and not insistent on her own way. Yet her birthing experience was a different issue. She needed to be the decision maker. Note the strength of her convictions after having given birth her own way. Also note her language. She regarded the traditional hospital birth as "surrender" and "giving in." When she talked about having chosen her own way of birth, however, her language was strong and proud. As denoted by her short, punctuated sentences, she was proud of having done it her way, unilaterally and uncontested.

CONTESTED BUT UNILATERAL CONTROL

In the second type of decision making, a unilateral decision was made by the care providers, but the women did not agree. They were placed in situations where, eventually, they had one of two responses: to (a) adapt or (b) refuse the care providers' interventions.

Contested but unilateral control: Decision making through eventual adaptation.

In the first example, a woman adapted to the decision of the care provider, but not without first objecting and trying to provide additional information for the physician's consideration. This woman wanted to avoid a glucose tolerance test during pregnancy when her urine specimen showed high sugar. She was opposed to having this test during pregnancy and explained that the glycosuria was due to what she had eaten prior to the visit. However, she reported that "he [the physician] wouldn't believe me. . . . So he made me go through [the test].." She considered herself a well-read noninterventionist, preferring fewer tests and procedures. Yet she stated that, when she discussed her understanding of various situations and treatments with providers, "they look at you like you've got three heads on your shoulders when you say something like that, because they don't think you know anything."

The second example was a woman who attempted to avert or postpone the physician's decision to perform a cesarean section. This example demonstrated the woman's request to labor longer, based on her mother's length of first labor. It included her critique of the physician's response.

> I had said to him, "can't I?" 'cuz I remember my mom, she had gone forty hours with her first, with my brother. And this was thirty-two [hours of labor], something like that. And I had said "can't I go eight more hours?" And he looked at me and he said, "well, you're only at three, do you really think eight more hours is going to do anything?" And I said "oh, okay, I guess not." He made me feel like the patient, unknowing, that I didn't have anything, I just felt like it was out of my hands . . . everything. They were just going to do to me what they want anyway. So, you know, it just made me feel really alone even more than I ever felt before. And so, anyway, we signed all the papers, crying and sobbing and hating every moment of it, and scared and, so I go in and have the C-section.

In this example, the care provider manipulated the decision, regardless of the woman's wishes. The woman complied, but note her response, her extreme emotional distress.

In the next example, the woman hoped to avoid an episiotomy and local anesthesia. Instead, she had to negotiate not only with the physician but with her partner as well. She capitulated to both, making a decision to please others while compromising what she wanted most, no anesthesia. In this unique situation, the woman had to mediate between her physician's and her partner's differing opinions on an episiotomy. She clearly expressed her concern: she hated needles; therefore, she did not want a local anesthetic before an episiotomy. Both she and her partner had talked to the doctor about not doing an episiotomy; the physician agreed to wait a few contractions, but explained to them that tearing was "worse." In this case, the woman became a mediator between the doctor and her partner while the baby's head was crowning:

> At one point he, the doctor, wanted to give me the shot to freeze, the local anesthesia, 'cuz he was planned on cutting me. And [my partner] immediately stopped. And no, I said, I don't want him to, a needle. And the doctor goes "Well?" And I said, "well maybe we don't have to have an episiotomy." And the doctor goes, "but if you tear, it's worse," and all this stuff. And I said, it was my whole fear of the needle again. So I said okay. So I get the shot, and, this was all during the pushing, I'm sure, and at one point he was going to cut. And [my partner] stopped him. He said well maybe she doesn't have to, can't we wait a. . . . And I wasn't saying anything because I could care less if he cuts me. By this time I could care less [after receiving the injection of local anesthetic]. [My partner]'s all concerned. He felt that doctors are too easily to cut, you know. You know, just so it doesn't, they're not there forever. And, so I said "couldn't we wait a few more pushes" then, just to try and be the mediator between [my partner] and the doctor, because [my partner] was about ready to come out and say "no, you're too fast, quick to cut." And so we did a few more pushes, and I, I remember the doctor saying, "you're gonna tear," and I could feel myself I was gonna tear. I said okay. Snip. And he did. And I think I had less stitches than normal. And I think if we had allowed him to cut when he first wanted to, I would have had as many stitches as the average person. . . . I guess I knew it would be inevitable that the doctor would cut. Just 'cuz I didn't want to be there forever either. And I knew I didn't want to tear, but I didn't want to be cut a lot, you know, if it wasn't necessary."

In these examples of contested decision making, the women adapted and submitted to the care providers' directives. The women stated that the providers did not value the women's knowledge. Note that the women reacted with a range of emotional responses, from quiet resignation to anger. Their sentences were not full of pride; in fact, they were still recounting their stories with anger and resentment, as if their births had occurred the day before. Notice they also used elongated sentences, as if simpler language was not enough to convey the depth of their feelings.

Contested but unilateral control:
Decision making through eventual refusal.

In this type of decision making, the care provider's unilateral decision was contested, and the woman planned to refuse care. A situation anticipated by one experienced mother was that if the laboratory personnel had insisted on trying repeatedly to obtain a blood sample from her baby's heel, she was going to refuse care. The woman stated, "I was gonna tell them how to do it right or I wasn't going to have it done."

Another woman contested the medical management of an earlier birth. She reported that she was upset about the treatment she had received from her elderly general practitioner and about the care she had received at the hospital. The treatment and care had included physician orders for a routine pubic area shave and an enema on admission, as well as an eventual cesarean section delivery followed by a separation from her family and baby. She therefore refused to see the same physician for a subsequent birth:

> I didn't want to. I couldn't go to the general practitioner again, and I didn't. I didn't want to go to [the hospital, named]. I just, the experience was too bad. I never wanted to go in that hospital again. And so I didn't really know where to go.

Instead, she sought midwifery care, using a word-of-mouth network to find local midwives. Thus she unilaterally and effectively refused physician care.

When unilateral decisions were made by the care providers but contested by the women, the women either resigned themselves to the intervention or they refused (or intended to refuse) care. The latter frequently resulted in an adversarial situation. Both scenarios evoked strong emotions in the women. Unilateral decisions made by providers are powerful methods of control and need to be acknowledged as such by health care professionals.

Shared Control

The third type of decision making was shared between the woman and the care provider. There were two ways that decisions were shared: (a) by explanations given by the care provider to the woman and (b) by requests made by either the woman or the care provider. In both instances, the woman was involved in the decision making and could make informed choices, even about unwanted procedures.

Shared control: Decision making through the use of explanation.

In this example, the woman was provided with explanations by her care providers. In her interview she made some comparisons between her two hospital births:

> The baby was not in distress at all; he was taking this really good. His heart rate was really excellent; everything was fine with him. I didn't want an internal fetal monitor either. I just didn't want that. I didn't know they screwed it into the head the first time, so I didn't want that with him. And that was fine. Anything I told them that I didn't want, I gave them a reason for why I didn't want it, and they were more than happy to, they didn't make me feel like I didn't know anything. They honored my wishes, and if they disagreed with it, they would just explain why they disagreed with it. And then I would just think, well, let's weigh the facts here then. Okay, okay, you know, all right, then that I suppose would be acceptable. But it was just the involvement was great, that I wasn't just having it done to me, that I did have a choice.

While the focal point of this quotation was avoiding the fetal scalp lead, the emphasis was on the shared decision making. The care providers listened, gave input, and planned with the mother, rather than excluding her. Note not only the woman's use of superlatives, such as "great" and "excellent," but the way in which she actively engaged in the decision making as an informed consumer.

In another example, a woman explained to her physician about her past history with pregnancy laboratory results. She reminded her physician of her tendency to have false results on urine pregnancy tests, thus averting a potentially harmful intervention when she was actually pregnant:

They told me for three months that I wasn't pregnant, because urine tests don't work on me. And they were gonna give me medicine to force me to have a period after the, during the third time that they ran a test to see if I was pregnant with this pregnancy. They said I wasn't pregnant; they were gonna give me medicine to force me to have a period. And I reminded the [care provider] about the first time I was pregnant; I didn't get a positive urine test until I was four months pregnant. And he did the blood test and it came back positive the next day. He told me not to take the medicine over the phone, to come in for the ultrasound. That it's just, it's really goofy how my body seems to constantly prove modern medical technology wrong. And they can run all the tests they want, and whatever their test results come up to, I would be tempted to believe just the opposite, because that's usually what it ended up coming up to anyway, is being about opposite of what they thought.

This woman negotiated and shared in decision making in a mutually productive manner. She took pride in the fact that her body defied modern technology and asserted that her knowledge of her own body transcended laboratory results.

Explanation as a method of negotiating decision making was a strong, positive approach when it was used by care providers or the women themselves. The women reported that they were being heard. Explanation and negotiated decision making did not generally evoke strong negative emotional responses, and in many cases, women or their care providers agreed willingly with a change in plan when presented with more information.

Shared control: Decision making through making requests.

In this type of decision making, the outcome was negotiated between the woman and her care provider by means of requests from either. A woman who had objected to the physician's internal examination expressed surprise that in a later home birth she had accepted a lay-midwife's offer of one:

I never imagined that I would want an internal examination except for with my fourth child, when it was offered, take it, take it or leave it. You know, whatever. It's not necessary. . . . She listened for her heartbeat and everything was fine, and I was fine, and so there was no medical reason that she should, you know, to determine anything more. . . . Except that, would I like to know how much further I have. And so, I'm still kind of surprised that I agreed to that, but knowing that it was her and how gentle she was, and how kind and I knew that, if there was any discomfort, no big deal, that's okay, no problem. It wouldn't have to continue. And she was quick, and, oh, I just, I was so comfortable with her. And so confident that she was very knowledgeable and would take care of any situation, any emergency situation.

The difference between the two situations for this woman was that the lay-midwife offered her the choice of an examination. The woman also perceived the exam as gentle, and she knew she could stop the examination if necessary. She could then accept the exam in order to gain some information about her progress.

Another woman reported that she had permitted a medical student to attend her first birth. She stated that usually she would not have allowed a student: "I had a med student that had asked permission, which I didn't mind 'cuz he was so well mannered, usually I don't, you know." The difference for her was the well-mannered way in which he made the request.

Yet another woman, who had been taught not to question and therefore did not question professionals during her first labor, took a proactive position during a subsequent pregnancy. She explained to her care provider that she appreciated information, for example, the results of examinations. She requested information this time instead of adhering to "this save-your-patient business," which she defined as withholding results to avoid upsetting the patient. She stated her beliefs because she needed to be involved in and experience her own emotions during labor. Birth was much more to her than an activity of one organ in her body. The care provider agreed with her request, informing her about antepartal testing and allowing her to refuse some tests.

This same woman requested a paracervical block (the injection of local anesthesia into the vagina next to the cervix to numb pelvic sensations in the lower abdomen) soon after hospital admission. She had discussed this plan in advance with her providers. She received two blocks within about an hour of each other, receiving the second after the first block was no longer effective in giving her pain relief. When the second paracervical block wore off, a nurse suggested an epidural. The woman (and her partner) emphasized how the nurse left the decision to them and gave them discussion time:

So I tried walking with that, but that started hurting too much, even with the [paracervical block], and it was just wearing on me. . . . I was whimpering, and things just weren't working out. And I think I laid down after that. And then the nurse, [name], she came in to talk to me about a spinal that they could give me, kind of like a half spinal . . . just so it would numb the pain. And then if I would end up having a C-section, then it would be already in place for it. And she said, "Now I'm not trying to push you into this. . . . I know you're in pain. . . . I know it's, your judgment isn't right [when in pain]." And she said, "But you just think about it. . . . I'll come back." She even let us think about it for a while. It was great. And we talked about it, and figured this was probably our best option. . . . So she came back, and then she called the anesthesiologist.

The sharing of information and the fact that the couple were allowed to make the final decision after the nurse's recommendation were important to this woman.

In summary, shared decision making required either that the care provider give information to the woman or that the woman or the care provider make a request for information, the goal being informed decision making. In most of the aforementioned examples, the women accepted the care providers' suggestions and felt good about the decisions. In all of these examples, the women and their providers shared the decision making. As a result, women in this study recounted powerful and positive responses to their birthing experiences.

SUSPENDED CONTROL: DECISION MAKING THROUGH WAITING WHEN UNSURE

The fourth and final type of decision making was to make no decision at all; that is, the woman and/or provider chose to wait and see what would happen. The women most commonly reported this form of decision making about signs of early labor or during times when slower changes were occurring.

For example, one woman reported waiting for definite signs that her contractions were indeed labor. Her partner expected her to know definitively because the contractions were occurring in her body. Although she was not immediately certain, in retrospect she reported a number of other body signs that were indicative of early labor: (a) pulling sensations in her lower pelvic muscles, (b) occasional contractions changing to more frequent and regular ones, and (c) increasing discomfort while trying to relax in the bathtub. When her bag of water ruptured, she could definitively state she was in labor: "It was warm, gushy, liquid, it was perfect. I'd never felt that before because they were ruptured by someone before. So this was new for me. And I thought, gee this is it! My water bag, there's no turning back now." Without that sign, she remained unclear about the numerous messages she reported receiving from her body. Hers was a decision to wait and make no decisions.

In another example, the woman called the nurse-midwife early in labor, and they waited together for labor to progress. The midwife supported waiting, encouraging the women verbally without making any active management decisions:

> She would say stuff like "Well, the baby's head is molding, you know, [participant's name]. It takes those babies a long time to mold, and it's going to be good if it can mold like that. . . . She was just real good about saying, "Oh, now this contraction's over, and you won't have to go through that contraction ever again, take them one at a time." . . . What helped the most was all the encouragement, all the pep talk. . . . Every time the contractions got harder I thought about taking medicine, but, you know, every time somebody would encourage me to go on and that I was making progress, and take one contraction at a time. And I just would do it, I would just follow what they said. . . . I would just think, well okay, take one more contraction and see how you feel, take one more contraction, see how you feel, and then I would get going for a while.

The use of encouraging statements by care providers was viewed as helpful by all of the women who participated in this study. The statements helped the women feel better about their progress while waiting for changes to occur. The statements also conveyed that the women could indeed cope with their labors even while awaiting progressive change. Eventually, labor circumstances would alter so that the woman or provider responded by making a decision. This decision making through waiting when unsure was employed when there was no particular urgency. It allowed more data to be gathered and evaluation to occur.

The negotiations in the birth stories were complex, but generally the women in this study wanted to be included in the decisions made about them; that is, they wanted to feel in control. Although women expressed their desires to be decision makers during labor, they reported that they were more often the recipients of others' control, particularly when providers insisted on routine protocols without allowing women to participate in their own care. When this occurred, the women reported feeling angry, hurt, or sad. Conversely, when given explanations and allowed simple choices even about the timing of unwanted or uncomfortable interventions, the women were more willing to accept technology or other interventions. Despite wanting to be participants in decision making, the women rarely expressed the desire to make all the decisions. They sought professionals for their knowledge and expertise but expected the professionals to solicit their perspectives and embodied information in return. In sum, women wanted their views respected and included in the planning that affected them and their infants.

RESISTING A CULTURE OF CONTROL

The women in this study clearly desired caring behaviors during their labors. This finding echoed the WHO recommendations for noninterventive, patient, and supportive care for women during normal labor. To achieve their wishes, however, the women often found themselves having to resist the culture of control. The foundational assumption of the culture of control—that is, that professionals possess superior knowledge—ignores three important dimensions: (a) that professionals often lack training and experience with normalcy, (b) the fact that the professionals lack the embodied knowledge of each woman experiencing her unique labor and birth, and (c) the special knowledge that develops from the lifelong commitment to the health of their offspring that parents bring to the birthing event. As Jordan (1997) asserted, a body of authoritative knowledge that is held separately by professionals is not inherently superior. In fact, it may be less useful if it is context-stripped of the woman's particular situation and her embodied information. Mutually sharing and respecting the contributions of providers and laboring women is preferred.

Women knew that the culture of control was not necessary, that it should be avoided and replaced with shared participation. Several of the women in my study reported the possibility of alternative scenarios. In the following example, one woman expressed her reactions when she realized, in retrospect, that important information was withheld from her that would have helped her cooperate with the physician's commands to push. Instead, she reported being so irritated with her provider's instructions that she wanted to hit her doctor:

He kept hollering at me that I had to push harder, I had to push harder for the baby. And he just kept frustrating me and angering me by . . . hollering this at me. And I didn't know why he was hollering that at me, and I just, I got to the point of being frustrated that I just wanted to [hit him]. But [Partner] had told me later on after the [care provider] had gone home and I got moved into the other room that it was because there had been [meconium, a sign that the fetus may have undergone some stress]. . . . He just thought the baby had to get out faster than I probably might have done it otherwise. . . . I didn't know about the [meconium] until after he was born and the [care provider] had gone back home. . . . I probably wouldn't have gotten angry. I probably would have just tried pushing harder than I already was. This is about the only thing I think I would have changed.

According to this woman, communication would have helped her participate more readily in pushing efforts and contribute toward her baby's delivery, rather than expending energy on anger. Her analysis of this event was not unlike that of others who provided alternative views on the presumed superiority of professionals' knowledge. When providers demanded controlling interventions, such as EFM or a woman's elimination, the women were angry. When providers informed and involved women in the decision making, the women were satisfied and sometimes elated with their births.

Women also knew that the culture of control did not result in providers readily listening to and respecting women's desires for their own births. Women often got caught between others' views and had to try to satisfy others' wishes rather than their own. Recall a previous example in which a woman had to meditate between the physician, her partner, and her own wishes. Eventually this woman adapted to the physician performing the episiotomy. However, her need to mediate between the provider's decision and her partner's desire illustrated what can happen in the environment where provider control is normative and involvement of the woman and family members is minimal. She capitulated to the demands of others, trying to please everyone but herself. Such negotiation was a remarkable feat for a laboring woman with a crowning infant. Yet, it may occur more often than health care providers acknowledge.

In another example, a woman reported a difficult interaction about an uncomfortable vaginal examination with a rural physician attending her home birth. She reported the events that occurred and her later reflections about the amount of effort she expended to modulate her own feelings while apologizing to him for her honest reaction and expression of pain. Her report included his insistence on the necessity of the vaginal examination to determine if there was a problem. She recalled that she was complaining about hurting and was troubled by the need to change her position in order to be examined. The tape she referred to in this quotation was her own tape recording of her labor and delivery:

He came in and he said "Hi, how is everything going?" You know, "How are you doing," and I said "I'm fine, I'm about to have the baby." And he said "Okay, let me have a look." And so I had to be turned around and sort of be on my back again, which was not at all comfortable. And he put his hand inside, you know, he was just doing a vaginal. He wanted to see, you know, if everything's okay. I understand that. But, it was so uncomfortable, and I said, "Please don't do that, it hurts." And then I said, "Please don't do that. It hurts!" And he said, he didn't say anything, he just got up and sat down. And I thought everything was fine. And I got back into my position, and I wasn't paying much attention to him, and I was having a baby, and he ah, what did I say? I was still kind of trying to get in position. I said, "Something doesn't feel quite right." And he said "Well, you wouldn't let me, you know, have a look." I mean, you know, maybe something is wrong. I said, "No, no, no, nothing's wrong." You know, I didn't feel that something was wrong. I just needed to move around a little bit and I was just saying it out loud. And then I thought, Oh!, I offended him when I told him I was uncomfortable. . . . And after I listened to this [tape recording of the birth], I thought, how, why was I so polite? I was giving birth! My goodness, he was actually unpleasant a couple times, just in this real short time that he was there. Two minutes, or one or two minutes. . . . On the tape that I listened to later, I was apologizing to him . . . when I said, "Please don't do that, it hurts, please don't do that, it *hurts*, don't do that." You know, and I thought, well, nothing of that at that moment. But later when I realized that it, you know, had ruffled his feathers, I was saying things like . . ."I'm sorry, it just was really uncomfortable in that it was unbearable for me right then." I couldn't, I could not [believe], you know, I was explaining why I had been sort of abrupt. But I thought that a woman in labor could sort of do that. You know, without anybody's feelings being hurt, you know, that that was just sort of given. But he, apparently, he apparently was, was miffed.

This women deferred to the presumed superiority of the physician's knowledge and authority by apologizing for asserting her needs.

As this and other examples illustrate, women recognized that the culture of control was not site specific; it occurred in both hospital and home births. In the birth narratives, control appeared to be linked more to the attitudes of the caregivers, regardless of the environment in which they practiced. Yet the culture of control was particularly prevalent in the hospital births, as evidenced in the prior example of the woman who compared her hospital cesareans with her home VBAC. Surrender, in her view, resulted in the providers making management decisions. Because the culture of control is more firmly entrenched or institutionalized in hospitals, this woman remained "in charge" of her birth and her decisions by having her next birth at home, where she was the knowledgeable one in her own environment.

Thus, women knew that altering the environment (from hospital to home) and the provider (from physician to lay midwife) could contribute to a substantive change in the culture. During one woman's home birth, she reported different experiences than those that often occurred in hospital births. This woman described a series of helpful activities that the lay-midwife provider performed: (a) spoke to the woman "like I was important," (b) inquired about the laboring woman's feelings, (c) offered to do an internal examination but only if the laboring woman wanted it, (d) "hummed with me inside, breathing along with me, just kind of helping me push and open," (e) reassured her that she was making progress and that labor would end, and (f) offered to assist her to a position in which she could have her baby born into her own hands. This informant attributed the latter offer to the lay-midwife's having connected with her, successfully picking up cues about her desires during their prior conversations and following through with well-timed questions in labor. As the woman reported, "she thought to ask me if I wanted to change my position [at the correct time to enable this child to be] born in a way that was special for me. I really appreciated that."

Still another woman who used a midwife reported the shared work of giving birth among herself, the lay midwife, and her assistant. The woman stated that she had done the work but that they had contributed a knowledge that she, in turn, could trust:

I was so thankful to [the lay midwife] and [the assistant] . . . to be there, you know, and what they do. How they, why they do what they do, and their reasons for doing it, and what they do for women, as far as being a midwife and having this knack, need, to be there for people. To me, at that point, I thanked them for every part of their life and for being there for me at that point, because it was great. 'Cuz yeah, I gave birth, but it couldn't have been done without somebody right there, you know. In today's day and age you just don't go and do those things alone, you know. You're too well educated to, you know, about the medical things, and you need somebody there to, to say, yeah, this is normal, this is okay, no this isn't, or, you know, something. So, yeah, it couldn't have been really done without their knowledge there. Yeah, I did it myself, but they helped make it beautiful, you know. And, 'cuz I wouldn't have known that I was hemorrhaging or that I wasn't. And I wasn't. I didn't lose much blood at all, they said. And after I asked them, is everything okay with the blood, you know, am I hemorrhaging or whatever? "No, you're fine, you didn't lose hardly anything." I thought, okay, everything's fine now, I can breathe easy and enjoy, 'cuz I was worried about that.

This woman relied on the providers' knowledge to reassure herself, but clearly she also relied on her own strengths.

The women in the study also reported that certified nurse-midwives (CNMs) helped alleviate the culture of control, sharing information with women without imposing directions, albeit in a hospital environment. One woman informant reported feeling understood when explanations from her CNM providers included sensations that she experienced. These details helped her during a difficult part of second-stage pushing. The woman reported that when she had an anterior lip of cervix remaining, the CNM offered to slide it past the baby's head so that the woman could be completely dilated and begin pushing. The CNM told the woman she would feel better when pushing. The woman was concerned that moving the cervix would hurt, and she stated that it did. She also reported that pushing did not feel better, just "different." However, the CNM supported her upper leg, instructed her in what position to use, gave her sips of water between contractions, and continued to make encouraging comments on her progress. The woman reported that these actions were very helpful. She continued:

[The nurse-midwife] was putting hot compresses on my hemorrhoids, my hemorrhoids hurt so bad. And it was, it was almost worse for her to touch. . . . The hot compress would feel good for a while, but then I could just feel this pressure on my hemorrhoid, and pressure from the inside from the baby, pressure from the [CNM]. And I knew she needed to put her hand somewhere close to my perineum to support it, but . . . it was a lot of pain. . . . So that [repeated encouragement about progress] kept me going. And I knew there wasn't any way out of this except to push the baby out. So then finally we got to the point where my perineum was stretching out, and that was beginning to burn. And it was really funny, like, right when I had this burning all the way around, then [the other CNM] said, "Oh, now you're probably going to have this feeling of a ring of fire. And it was just exactly that contraction that I was pushing on when she told me that. It was just like she knew exactly what I was feeling. . . . That was nice to have her, you know, like, acknowledging my feelings. And then I didn't have to do so much complaining. Let's see, then I would blow a bit whenever I, whenever I felt that burning feeling.

This woman reported various actions of certified nurse-midwives that assisted and supported her during second-stage pushing. She used the nurse-midwife's knowledge but also relied on her own. Most women reported that nurse-midwives' actions were helpful, particularly those that acknowledged the women's sensations. When women were included in decisions and received assistance and explanations (including experiential sensations) without control, they felt confident about their own abilities and positive about the birth experience.

In general, the midwives did not have as many examples of unilateral control attributed to them by the women. Similarly, nurse-midwives who functioned in hospitals did not manifest the culture of control. Instead, in the examples that included midwives, women reported that they usually shared decision making. In the prior examples of midwife care providers, the women stated that all the midwives contributed essential work to their safe deliveries. Without the midwives' presence and the sharing of their wisdom, the women reported that they would not have had the confirmatory explanations that contributed to their positive outcomes. In the women's views, they had done the work of birthing, but the midwives had enhanced their experiences, staying with the women and helping to make the experience satisfying through the application of midwifery wisdom.

Based on my research with women's birth narratives, I believe that control of decision making is a major issue that affects birthing women and the courses of their labors. This belief was echoed by the international WHO statement and analyses of evidence-based practices, which recommended limiting technology while increasing supportive care. This belief was also echoed by the women in this study, who demonstrated that if decisions about women and their infants were made jointly between women and their providers, the result would be better outcomes, both physically and emotionally.

BUILDING A CULTURE OF RECIPROCITY

In the final level of analysis in my study, the coders and I identified interpretive statements that represented distillations of the women's meanings across their birth stories. These distilled statements included the women's convictions that providers and women should share their power, that is, mutually contribute their data, knowledge, and experience. Better outcomes (e.g., healthier infants and more positive experiences) resulted when decision making was shared and all parties were fully informed; more negative outcomes (e.g., women feeling hurt and angry) resulted when decisions were unilaterally made by care providers. The women in my study wanted a common goal acknowledged: providers and parents all want healthy outcomes for the women and for the infants. This shared goal could provide the common ground wherein women and their care providers create a culture of reciprocity.

To build a culture of reciprocity, I offer the aggregated responses of the women in my study as foundational claims:

1. My body is a powerful means, instrumental to making a new human life, and we need to use this power wisely to have this baby well.
2. I am responsible for my body and my choices throughout this pregnancy, labor, delivery, and family relationship building.
3. I will love and raise this baby as part of my family for the rest of our lives.
4. I will bring people with me to support me through this life-changing event.
5. I know myself, my life experiences, and my body sensations, living inside them; you must listen to me to know my valuable data.
6. I chose you as care provider, therefore you must work with me.
7. You as provider have knowledge and power that can help me through the unknown parts of the pregnancy, labor, and delivery.
8. You as provider have technology that you can use; I want it used sparingly as needed in my individual situation, not because the use of technology is widespread and routine for others.

9. There is a holiness, sacredness, or spirituality to birth. I want it respected, not violated.
10. I will not ever forget this birth experience.
11. When we share the power we each have and mutually contribute to data-based, knowledge-based, experience-based decisions, we produce a healthier baby.
12. When you impose your power on my experience, I am irritated (angry, hurt) by not being included or fully valued for my contributions, plus sometimes your powerful interventions can hurt my baby.
13. I have additional unstated power: I can go elsewhere for care in the future; I could even sue you for malpractice.
14. However, we have a common goal: a healthy outcome. I would prefer to work together toward our goal throughout pregnancy, labor, and delivery.
15. Our work is reciprocal; for example, when you as provider have improved the birthing environment and support, I have felt more competent about my own birth-giving.

Basically, the women said they wanted more access and more rights to their own birth experiences and their own interpretations of them. Clearly, in these distilled meanings, women did not desire a culture of control. They have described a desire for a culture of reciprocity with shared knowledge and power.

IMPLICATIONS FOR CAREGIVERS ABOUT CONTROL

Various researchers have confirmed laboring women's expressed desire that they receive information and that their views be heard and considered by their care providers. Analyzing the "informational politics" between sixteen women and their care providers via in-depth interviews, Brown (1996) concluded that the level of communication between a woman and her care provider is affected by technology and by how the care providers manage it. The women in Brown's study preferred an open flow of communication; however, care providers could facilitate or obstruct this communication, based on how they related to the women. For example, applying technology marginalized women's involvement in their births and, as a result, contributed to poorer communication. Brown's results supported earlier studies. Analyzing videotapes of second-stage labor,

McKay and Smith (1993) identified communication as a major theme in women's birth experiences. The women in this study wanted both information sharing and a high quality of exchange between themselves and their care providers, with *quality* meaning shared decision making, rather than unilateral communication from the provider to the woman in labor.

Whether or not women's expressed desire for communication and shared decision making occurs can affect the birth experience. DiMatteo, Kahn, and Berry (1993) reported that when a desired level of communication was not achieved between women and their care providers, two themes—lost autonomy and lost control—dominated new mothers' birth narratives. DiMatteo, Kahn, and Berry also reported that when satisfactory communication was achieved—that is, when providers listened to women and respected their emotional, informational, and self-determination needs—then positive effects ensued. Similarly, Seguin et al. (1989) identified the most significant components in women's satisfaction with their birth experience. Analyzing a questionnaire given to 1,790 Montreal women after giving birth, the researchers concluded that the most significant component in women's satisfaction with care from physicians was participation in the decision-making process and that the most significant component in women's satisfaction with care from nurses was receiving information. Brown and Lumley (1994) reported similar survey results: 790 Australian women reported overall greater dissatisfaction with their intrapartum care than with their prenatal care. The women expressed greater satisfaction when they received information, participated in decision making, and formed relationships with their providers.

The challenge to care providers is to implement the knowledge gained in research by involving women more actively in information sharing and decision making, which affect women's labors and births, and infants' health. Women's views need to be central in the conduct of labor and birth. A woman's role in her own birth should be that of star, prominent and center stage (Hanson, VandeVusse, and Harrod 2001). Maternal involvement in decision making during labor and birth is what women desire. Professional knowledge and power should be used to support, not control, birth processes. Unilateral control should be avoided. When laboring women are provided with information and involved in discussions and planning their care, they are much more likely to feel positive and less likely to express negative emotions such as anger or hurt. Simkin

(1996) and Rothman (1996) emphasized the importance of the woman feeling important, strong, trusted, and competent. If these powerful and positive emotional consequences emerge before, during, and after birth, they have a lifelong impact on women's self-images and on their abilities to mother effectively (Simkin 1991).

Given the overwhelming evidence in these studies, caregivers must rethink birth from women's points of view. VandeVusse (1999b) analyzed women's birth stories and identified many important forces that had exerted control and thereby affected the women's experiences. External forces, such as providers and procedures, predominated, but forces internal to the woman were also powerful influences. Labor is a highly complex process with multiple interacting effects. As the women's distilled meanings indicated, mutuality among all those involved in labor, dealing respectfully with each other and the process while sharing in decision making, will promote a culture of reciprocity. When women participate fully in decisions about birth, it is possible that their input will help limit the excessive use of interventions. Providers will no longer apply technology routinely, but only after evaluating individual situations and deciding with each woman to use only the technology deemed necessary. This selective and reasoned use of interventions will help to meet the WHO guidelines, while contributing to improved maternal and infant outcomes. Another benefit will be better control of escalating costs, thereby limiting unnecessary technology use and its oftentimes expensive by-products, such as increased cesarean sections. Therefore, the collective work of providers, women, and society is to resist technology-mediated provider control with its related enforcement of women's passivity in labor. Instead, providers must work closely with women to meet their unique needs in labor. The projected benefits are many, including that each woman could become the central focus during the birth process. This could reverse the marginalization of her importance that currently occurs whenever superior professional knowledge is assumed and technology and interventions are routinely used.

As beginning steps, caregivers need to understand the negative effects of the culture of control as well as the possibilities of a culture of reciprocity. To achieve such understanding, caregivers can commit to using sound research evidence, to questioning the application of technology in normal birth, to employing shared decision making, and to valuing women's birth narratives. The resulting understanding may help caregivers change practices not only in ways that benefit women and promote healthier birth outcomes but also in ways that help health care personnel develop further as practitioners. Such changes would foster a culture of reciprocity—a culture that better supports the natural processes of birthing while helping to realize a partnership between professionals and laboring women.

REFERENCES

Albers, L. L., and D. A. Savitz. 1991. Hospital setting for birth and use of medical procedures in low-risk women. *Journal of Nurse-Midwifery* 36(6): 327–33.

Brown, C. 1996. Freedom of choice: An expression of emerging power relationships between a childbearing woman and her caregiver. *International Journal of Childbirth Education* 11(3): 12–16.

Brown, S., and J. Lumley. 1994. Satisfaction with care in labor and birth: A survey of 790 Australian women. *Birth* 21(1): 4–13.

Davis-Floyd, R. 1986. Routine and rituals in childbirth: A new view. *NAACOG Update Series*, vol. 5, lesson 10. Princeton, N.J.: Continuing Professional Education Center.

———. 1992. *Birth as an American rite of passage.* Berkeley: University of California Press.

DiMatteo, M. R., K. L. Kahn, and S. H. Berry. 1993. Narratives of birth and the postpartum: Analysis of the focus group responses of new mothers. *Birth* 20(4): 204–11.

Enkin, M., M. J. N. C. Keirse, J. Neilson, and M. J. Renfrew. 2000. *A guide to effective care in pregnancy and childbirth: A synopsis.* 3d ed. New York: Oxford University Press.

Goer, H. 1995. *Obstetric myths versus research realities: A guide to the medical literature.* Westport, Conn.: Bergin & Garvey.

Hanson, L., L. VandeVusse, and K. S. Harrod. 2001. The theater of birth: Scenes from women's scripts. *Journal of Perinatal and Neonatal Nursing* 15(2): 18–35.

Jordan, B. 1977. Authoritative knowledge and its construction. In *Childbirth and authoritative knowledge: Cross-cultural perspectives*, ed. R. E. Davis-Floyd and C. F. Sargent, 55–79. Berkeley: University of California Press.

McKay, S., and S. Y. Smith. 1993. "What are they talking about? Is something wrong?" Information sharing during the second stage of labor. *Birth* 20 (3): 142–47.

Mitford, J. 1992. *The American way of birth.* New York: Dutton.

Rooks, J. P. 1997. *Midwifery and childbirth in America*. Philadelphia: Temple University Press.

Rothman, B. K. 1996. Women, providers, and control. *Journal of Obstetric, Gynecologic, and Neonatal Nursing* 25(3): 253–56.

Seguin, L., R. Therrien, F. Champagne, and D. Larouche. 1989. The components of women's satisfaction with maternity care. *Birth* 16(3): 109–13.

Simkin, P. 1991. Just another day in a woman's life: Women's long-term perceptions of their first birth experience. Part 1. *Birth* 18(4): 203–10.

———. 1996. The experience of maternity in a woman's life. *Journal of Obstetric, Gynecologic, and Neonatal Nursing* 25(3): 247–52.

Stein, J., and P. Y. Su, eds. 1980. *The Random House dictionary*. New York: Ballantine.

Supplee, R. B., and T. M. Vezeau. 1996. Continuous electronic fetal monitoring: Does it belong in low-risk births? *MCN: The American Journal of Maternal/Child Nursing* 21:301–6.

Thacker, S. B., and D. F. Stroup. 2000. Continuous electronic fetal monitoring for fetal assessment during labor (Cochrane Review). In *The Cochrane Library*. Oxford: Update Software, Issue 2.

VandeVusse, L. 1999a. Decision-making in analyses of women's birth stories. Birth 26:43–50.

———. 1999b. The essential forces of labor revisited: 13 Ps reported in women's birth stories. *MCN: The American Journal of Maternal/Child Nursing* 24:176–84.

Wagner, M. 1994. *Pursuing the birth machine: The search for appropriate birth technology*. Camperdown, Australia: ACE Graphics.

World Health Organization, Technical Working Group. 1997. Care in normal birth: A practical guide. *Birth* 24(2): 121–23.

PARTNERS OR PATIENTS?

A Conclusion

Helen M. Sterk

The women with whom we spoke and to whom we listened asked only to be seen as partners in the process of giving birth, ones who hold a position of a certain level of privilege in relation with their caregivers, life partners, and babies. Instead, if they gave birth in a hospital, under typical obstetric care, they were seen as patients, who, for the good of their babies, needed to listen to doctors' orders. We urge listening to the women. As Leona Vande Vusse suggested in the preceding chapter, birthing care should defer to the women. After all, they are the ones doing hard, unusual, and important work. They are the ones who have unique access to their own experience of labor. And they are the ones who will be in relationship with that child once she or he is born. These are weighty reasons to place women at the center of attention in the situation of birth.

We also need to remember that women giving birth are not sick. They are engaged, instead, in a natural act, one their bodies are designed to do. Babies also are designed to be born. In Carla Hay's historical chapter, we discovered that doctors, over time, increasingly have framed birth as inherently risky, dangerous for both mother and child, even to the point of advocating technological intervention, as with forceps and cesarean surgeries, to "protect" them both. The point of view of birthing women as patients rather than partners was warranted by positioning the baby at the center of the process of labor and delivery. Decisions to use technology and invasive techniques, such as electronic fetal monitoring, forceps, episiotomies, cesarean surgeries, and so on, become easier to make when the baby and its health orient attention. After all, who would be "insane" enough to put a baby at risk?

And yes, the safety of the baby does matter, as does the safety of the mother. A good birth requires satisfactory outcomes (although just what constitutes satisfaction may vary from situation to situation and even person to person). Yet, as Carla Hay noted in the historical chapter, even in the seventeenth and eighteenth centuries, before birth technology was widely available, estimates say the mother died in only about 1 percent of the births. Now, even the most conservative statistics indicate fewer than 15 percent of births present levels of danger that would require medical interventions (Goer 1995). Korte and Scaer argue in *A good birth, a safe birth* that "The active management of all births is an invention of the [nineteen] seventies, long after the greatest decreases began and continued in maternal mortality" (1992, 102). As the technology grew, occasions for its use expanded, warranted by a rhetorical appeal to the safety of the baby. As Ivan Illich (1976) has argued in the case of medical practice and Jacques Ellul (1979) in the case of technology in general, humans have a tendency to defer to technology, seeing it as a kind of savior invoked in the name of the good, in this case, in the name of the best available medical practice.

Yet, insofar as birthing is concerned, the best available medical practice may involve the *least* use of technology. Numerous books and scholarly articles argue that birthing has been too highly managed (see the reference lists at the end of the chapters in this book). Technology is becoming its own reason for being, to the detriment of women and not to the significant betterment of healthy babies (Enkin, Keirse, and Chalmers 1989; Korte and Scaer 1992, 100–102; Goer 1995). In a sense, this book echoes all these others. However, our contribution is to provide a new set of reasons for reducing "high-tech" and increasing "low-tech" birthing. These reasons are grounded in the women's narratives that are told in the Birthing Project archive and represented here.

Narratives provide a kind of moral reasoning. They provide symbolic structures within which people test their perceptions of events and agents, either fictionally or actually. As Walter Fisher (1987) has argued, people use narrative to make sense of life. They look to how meaningfully the parts of the narrative fit together within itself (coherence) as well as to how faithful the narrative is to their lived experience (fidelity). Stories contain wisdom about human life. They show us the actions people take and the consequences of those actions. We draw conclusions from stories in deciding how to live our own lives. Krista Ratcliffe's chapter comparing and contrasting literary and lived birthing narratives shows well the ways in which these particular stories make some ideas about birth seem more normal, reasonable, and "sane" than others.

Almost all the birthing research with which I am familiar bases its reasoning on scientific, quantifiable research studies. These studies look at infant mortality, mothers' mortality, length of labor, and so on. These are things that can be seen and measured. Even research that critiques standard medical procedures in the case of birth, such as Korte and Scaer (1992), Goer (1995), Oakley (1980, 1984, 1992), and Mitford (1992), among others, does so on the basis of showing that scientific randomized, controlled trials (RCT) do not show better birth outcomes are a result of routine and aggressive use of technological interventions. I understand well why they focus on RCTs. They seek to convince medical practitioners to change, based on the practitioners' own sacred form of argumentation.

We, however, see the women. We take them at their word. Their narratives ground our arguments. In a very real sense, in this book, we present moral arguments for changing standard medical birthing practice and the policies that support them. We draw our reasons from the stories women told us about their bodies, the children that grew inside and came from them, and their experiences of controlling or reciprocating care.

We hold a speech act theory of meaning, in which meaning is understood as being created by an interaction of the expert's intentions, the message's components (in this case, all the possible ways "birth" can be done), and the uptake, the meaning attributed to the message by the one who receives it (Searle 1969; Austin 1972). In light of this theory, when it comes to birthing care, women need to play both the role of initiator of communication and that of listener. In either case, their point of view needs to be factored into any understanding of what giving birth means. Research that focuses on medical caregivers and their definitions of birthing through scientific RCTs leaves women's uptake out of consideration. Through considering women's stories on the meaning of birth, we contribute the element of humanity to arguments aimed at reducing the presumption carried by routine birthing interventions. Women must be considered as full partners if the complete meaning of birthing is to be uncovered. Women must not only receive but initiate meaning.

Very simply put, we have shown that women often feel themselves harmed emotionally, psychologically, socially, and spiritually by birthing practices that are unnecessarily invasive. The rhetoric of these practices figures women as if they were colonized peoples, to use Alice Kehoe's analogy, rather than knowledgeable agents who should be partners in decisions about practices that will be used on them. For the reason of harm to women, as well as the reason that invasive medical practices have not been proven to produce significantly different or better outcomes for either babies or women, we argue that a midwifery model should be instituted for all normal births in America.

Elements of this model have been contributed by the preceding chapters, especially Helen Sterk's on caring communication and Leona VandeVusse's on shared decision making. Here, we will suggest a set of related practices whose rhetoric and warranted actions would enhance the quality of birthing in America by placing women at the center, with caregivers figured as guides whose job is to help women to understand what their bodies are doing and to work with their bodies.

As both Carla Hay and Krista Ratcliffe suggest, two polarized models of birthing exist in America. The medical model holds the hegemonic position; while the natural model strongly opposes most elements of the medical model. When we refer to a medical model, we mean a model based on physician-defined control of birthing, which often legitimates the use of technological and pharmaceutical interventions in the natural process of birthing, on the grounds of the safety of the fetus, as that is defined by physicians (see chapter 4). On the other pole, a natural model is one that might be practiced by lay midwives in home births, one that would endorse mother-defined control of birthing, avoiding virtually all interventions (whether medical, technological, or pharmaceutical), on the grounds of the autonomy of the mother. The medical model figures women as patients, legitimately under the control of standardized birthing protocols, while the natural model presumes women to be agents, whose needs and desires should be accommodated.

In our view, the midwifery model operates from the assumption that women are partners with caregivers, occupying a middle ground, perhaps located somewhat closer to the natural than the medical model. In the midwifery model, perhaps it could be said that a good birth is the focus. What counts as a good birth will vary from woman to woman, depending on her comfort level with her own body and her need for reassurance that potential emergencies can be handled. An arrangement of persons and circumstances that fits the wants and needs of the woman and also respects the judgment of competent caregivers, we believe, will best fulfill the demands of a good birth. For some women, a good birth will require a hospital and a highly directive doctor. For some, it will call for a midwife attending the birth in a hospital. For some, it might mean getting out of the hospital setting entirely, being able to choose a free-standing birth center or one's own home, where midwives guide the birth. In any case, we advocate pairing birthing women with experienced caregivers, who can guide by using hands and words to reassure women and manage birth, who use drugs and technology only sparingly (adhering to what Lee H. called "minimal exposure" [Lee H. 1996, 20]), and whose sense of protocol is tempered by and oriented to women's needs and wants. This sort of care gives honor to women and also meets the needs of babies coming into the world. This sort of care implicitly says that birth is a normal human process, *and* that it needs to be respected as a highly meaningful act in the course of a birthing woman's life. She should not be robbed of her experience.

In order for a midwifery model to replace the current medical model, certain aspects of economics, setting, use of technology and drugs, and communication will need to be transformed. As noted above, the scientifically based arguments for these changes have been made well (see especially Goer 1995 and Korte and Scaer 1992). We argue that the transformation needs to come for scientific reasons, yes, but also for moral reasons. If the quality of birthing women's experience can be enhanced without threat to either maternal or fetal life, then it should become a priority to do so.

The first change needed involves the *economics of birthing*. Unless it is economically feasible for women to choose midwifery care, they will not choose it. Current insurance plans tend not to cover any means or place of birth other than those directed by doctors in hospitals. In order for women to have a range of options from which to choose, they need to know that the cost of care will be covered. If midwifery care is not covered under insurance, women need to pay for it out of their own, or their family's, resources. Perforce, then, midwifery care is marginalized, used only rarely, by women who have a certain amount of wealth. This is ironic because, in general, care by a midwife costs far less than that by a doctor. The women interviewed for the Birthing Project who had chosen midwives said the cost of midwifery care in their region of the country usually was about one-half or one-third the rate for doctor care. So, since it makes sense economically, for the safety of the baby (see Goer 1995 for a lengthy discussion of the medical literature's confirmation that midwife care actually promotes better outcomes for maternal and fetal safety), and for the good of the mother, midwifery care should be an option that routinely is paid for by health insurance.

The possible *sites for birthing* need to be expanded. Instead of being limited to choosing a maternity ward in a hospital, women should be able to choose among at least the following: the maternity ward, a birthing center located in a hospital, a free-standing birthing center, or home. Different women have different tolerances for settings. For some, unless they can be at home, they cannot relax. The context of a hospital, with its smells and associations with illness, scares them. Yet others feel more secure in a hospital, knowing they are right there by the technology that could save their lives or their babies in case of an emergency. Some may prefer the middle ground of a birthing center, where midwives direct the care. For some, a birthing center in a hospital offers the best of both worlds, while others prefer to be separated from the hospital entirely, so medical protocols will be less likely to be brought to bear. Again, just as women should be free to choose their caregivers, so they should be free to choose, with their caregivers, the sites for birth that best suit them. Health insurance plans should cover not only a range of caregivers, but also a range of sites.

No matter where birth takes place, no matter who manages or guides the birthing process, the *routine use of technology, drugs, and invasive techniques needs to be held to a standard of minimal exposure.* As the last three chapters have shown, women feel harm most keenly when their bodies are tethered to machines, limiting their movement, when they are cut off not only from pain but from all sensation by drugs, and when they are cut and pieced together without their consent. Yes, of course, there are times when emergencies present themselves, and in those cases, women's needs and desires take second place. Yet those times are rare. The great majority (85 percent according to most research consulted in this book) of births are not dangerous. In the medical parlance, they are "uneventful." However, the women we interviewed saw their birthings as among the *most* eventful things in their lives. In a woman's life, birth is not routine; it is filled with meaning. Standard care, we would argue, should be conducted in such a way to help women recognize what the birth means to them and encourage them to work with their own bodies to bring their babies into the world.

Certain very specific ways of doing these things exist. They require caregivers *to see women and babies as a unit.* What is good for the mother needs to be seen as good for the baby. Mothers should not be immobilized in order to be monitored for any potential emergency. It should be presumed that each birth will be a healthy, normal birth unless clear counterindications exist. Supportive, wait and see care during labor enhances understanding of the integration of mothers and babies. High touch, hands-on care during delivery does the same.

Supportive care during labor should include routine use of doulas. A doula is a woman whose job is to talk with and touch laboring women. The research of Bertsch et al. (cited in Kennell et al.) found that while male partners touched laboring women 20 percent of the time, doulas touched women 95 percent of the time. Doulas have given birth themselves and care about helping other women to have a satisfying birthing experience. Not a replacement for a woman's partner, a doula helps a woman to understand what her body is doing at a given moment and through which stage of labor she is moving. Scientifically based studies confirm the value of a doula. In a controlled study in a hospital comparing women who labored without doulas with those who had one, Kennell and associates found Pitocin was used on 43.6 percent of women without doula support and only 17 percent of those with such support; epidural anesthesia was used on 55.3 percent of those without and 7.8 percent of those with; forceps assisted deliveries on 26.3 percent of those without and 8.2 percent of those with; cesarean surgery occurred on 18 percent of those without and 8 percent of those with; fever occurred in mothers 10.3 percent of those without and 1.4 percent with; and sick newborns were found in 24 percent of those without and 10.4 percent of those with. These are extraordinary figures. If there were a drug or technology that had similar positive effects, it would be adopted immediately, no matter what the expense.

The women in the Birthing Project, many of whose stories are told in this book, narrated the harm caused them by procedures being imposed without their permission, informed consent, and sometimes even knowledge. Instead of working with the women, working with their bodies, caregivers worked against the grain of the women's knowledge, treating them as vessels only, not as persons who deserved to be consulted. Having a doula during labor, a person who belongs to them for the duration of the labor, who can ease the anxiety that may lead to clenching rather than opening up, does good things for women. If the presence of a doula can reduce so drastically the need for drugs, episiotomies, and cesarean surgeries, then using her services makes good sense all around. Adding a doula to the mix of caregivers, all of whom are there for the purpose of enabling women to birth babies, would make the process more integrated and less alienating, and thereby more under the control of the women.

Other high touch, low technology practices that would help women through labor and delivery, in a way that sees them as whole persons rather than as isolated body parts, include relying on time and the human body to do its work. This would require a change in protocols related to timing. Currently, medical protocols assume labor will last no more than twenty-four hours and the pushing stage no more than two hours (Korte and Scaer 1992; Goer 1995). We would argue that timing should be cued from individual women rather than a normal curve. Women, and their individual tolerances for labor and delivery, need to be seen as the orientation points, rather than statistical averages.

Techniques that encourage a woman's body to work at its peak during labor and delivery should be used. Women should be guided by their caregivers to seek ways to help their bodies work well during labor, such as walking, leaning, rocking, taking a shower, or sitting in a tub of warm water. Women do not labor efficiently if they are lying on their backs in bed, strapped to monitors, with intravenous needles lodged in their arms. Tethers to the bed may make life easier for caregivers who see women as vessels temporarily holding babies, but they do nothing to help laboring women see themselves as partners rather than patients. Instead of electronic fetal monitoring, intermittent auscultation (listening to the fetal heartbeat through a stethoscope) should be used routinely. During delivery, women should be encouraged to use positions that serve their bodies and their babies, not ones that make it easier for caregivers to see, manipulate, and cut women in order to pull out babies. In particular, we encourage the use of perineal massage in preparation for delivery to help women to relax and open up wide enough so that babies can be born without too much tearing and without the "help" of episiotomy cuts.

In summary, we endorse labor and delivery care that take its cue from women. This will require a repositioning of the key players in American birthing. Currently, the rhetoric of birthing puts babies and their safety at the center. This rhetoric masks the reality that doctors and medical protocols are at the center of birthing. When the needs of caregivers determine actions, the meaning of birth becomes impoverished. A rich, meaningful experience of birth will be made possible when the birthing unit of mother and baby takes central position in all decision making. In order for conditions to be created where that can happen, women who are giving birth need to be heard. To be full partners, women need to initiate talk and be listened to. Whatever needs to be done to situations, protocols, and people to make that happen should be done. Listening requires response tempered by what is heard. When caregivers' expertise partners with actions guided by women's responses, meaning will be enhanced, and when women are seen as having expertise and their messages are received with respect, quality of care will increase. The demands of morality in the birthing situation will then be met.

REFERENCES

Austin, J. L. 1972. *How to do things with words.* Oxford: Oxford University Press.

Ellul, J. 1979. *The technological society.* New York: Knopf

Enkin, M, J. N. C. Keirse, and I. Chalmers. 1989. *Effective care in pregnancy and childbirth.* Oxford: Oxford University Press.

Fisher, W. R. 1987. *Human communication as narration: Toward a philosophy of reason, value and action.* Columbia: University of South Carolina Press.

Goer, H. 1995. *Obstetric myths versus research realities: A guide to the medical literature.* Westport, Conn.: Bergin and Garvey.

Illich, I. 1976. *Medical Nemesis.* New York: Pantheon Books.

Kennell, J., Klaus, M., McGrath, S., Robertson, S., Hinkley, C. 1991. Continuous emotional support during labor in a U.S. hospital. *Journal of the American Medical Association* 265 (1 May): 2197–2201.

Korte, D, and R. Scaer. 1992. *A good birth, a safe birth.* Cambridge, Mass.: Harvard Common Press.

Lee H. 1996. Interview by Helen Sterk, 23 May. Available from Memorial Library Archives, Marquette University, Milwaukee, WI 53201.

Mitford, J. 1992. *The American way of birth.* New York: Dutton.

Oakley, A. 1980. *Women confined: Towards a sociology of childbirth.* New York: Schocken Books.

———. 1984. *The captured womb: A history of the medical care of pregnant women.* Oxford: Basil Blackwell.

———. 1992. *Social support and motherhood: The natural history of a research project.* Oxford: Basil Blackwell.

Searle, J. R. 1969. *Speech acts: An essay in the philosophy of language.* Cambridge: Cambridge University Press.

ABOUT THE AUTHORS

Helen M. Sterk is Professor of Communication Arts and Sciences, teaching gender, communication, and rhetoric at Calvin College. Her research specialization is women in popular culture.

Krista Ratcliffe is Associate Professor of English at Marquette University, and teaches writing, rhetorical theory, and women's literature. She specializes in women's rhetoric.

Carla H. Hay is Associate Professor of History at Marquette University and teaches American and European history, as well as women in western civilization. Her research specialty is political institutions and ideologies in domestic and imperial British communities.

Alice B. Kehoe is Professor Emeritus of Anthropology at Marquette University. She studies Native Americans in the northern United States and Canada.

Leona VandeVusse is Assistant Professor and Director of the Nurse-Midwifery Program at Marquette University. Her research focuses on obstetric nursing care and nurse-midwifery.